*Improving Writing
and Learning*

IMPROVING WRITING AND LEARNING

A Handbook for Teachers in Every Class

JUDITH BECHTEL
Northern Kentucky University

ALLYN AND BACON, INC.
Boston, London,
Sydney, Toronto

Library of Congress Cataloging in Publication Data

Bechtel, Judith.
  Improving writing and learning.

  Bibliography: p.
  Includes index.
  1. English language—Composition and Exercises.
2. Report writing. 3. Research. I. Title.
LB1631.B37 1985   808'.042'07   84-14470
ISBN 0-205-08201-7

Printed in the United States of America

10 9 8 7 6 5 4 3 2 1 89 88 87 86 85 84

Contents

3

Assessment of Student Writing Ability   30

4

Record-Keeping Tasks   57

5

Research Papers   78

6

Essay Tests   113

7

Creative Writing   131

8

Evaluation of Student Writing   152

9

Establishing a School-Wide Writing Program   181

Preface

A revolution has occurred in the teaching of writing. Beginning in 1969 with the publication of Janet Emig's *The Composing Processes of Twelfth Graders*, there has been a resurgence of interest in research about writing. Spurred on by British researchers at the University of London (most notably, James Britton and the London Schools Council), graduate students and teachers in America began looking closely at the behaviors of student writers. A whole new specialty was born—that specialty within the discipline of English called "Composition."

What we now know about writing and how it is learned make obsolete the ways most of us were taught. We now know that writing is a wonderfully recursive process involving alternating stages of thinking, drafting, revising, and editing. The different stages require different mind-sets, too, and being critical at the early stages can be terribly inhibiting, especially for the inexperienced writer. The tradition of red-marking student papers most assuredly has had an inhibiting effect on student writers.

Another tradition which may have hindered more than helped is the tradition of teaching grammar, punctuation, and other discrete subskills out of context. It seems evident that students only learn to write by actually writing—and this only after they have had wide-ranging exposure to the written code through extensive reading.

But for the purposes of this book the most marvelous implication of the new research in composition involves the close tie between writing and learning. Whereas formerly we thought of writing as a medium for communicating what had already been learned, we now see it as a powerful mode of discovering meaning. Thus writing activities are appropriate—even necessary—in all courses.

Teachers of science, social studies, math, and other subjects will find this book useful as a guide for encouraging more writing in their various courses. English teachers, too, will find this book useful. By thinking of writing in a new way, by assigning it in smaller and less formal doses, all teachers will find that writing is a very palatable medicine indeed. I have taken special care to present ideas and suggestions in a step-by-step manner. From past experience I know that teachers are too busy to take on extraneous work, especially if they don't see direct indications of better learning of the information and concepts of their discipline. Many teachers who have tried the ideas described here report not only that more learning has occurred in their classes, but also that morale has improved. Excitement and involvement accompany this new approach to writing and learning. Students report that they have actually come to like writing more from having had to do more of it.

One reason for this excitement about writing is that the approach advocated here is grounded in a whole theory of learning, an approach based on the realization that people yearn to make meaning. Once constant and natural and informal writing is recognized as central to the development of more sophisticated or polished prose, then using writing and teaching through writing begin to make sense. On the other hand, many in-service programs for teachers and other earnest endeavors to counter the so-called literacy crisis flounder because they are not grounded in good theory. Although teachers prefer something practical and seemingly abhor the purely theoretical, well-tested lesson plans cannot make up for the lack of a viable theoretical base. James Britton and the London Projects offer such a base, yet their work has not been applied on a large scale within the American educational establishment.

In describing these writing activities and explaining the theory upon which they are based, I am especially grateful to my friends and colleagues at Northern Kentucky University who tried many of them as part of the interdisciplinary courses sponsored by a grant from the National Endowment for the Humanities in 1981, also to Toby Fulwiler, formerly of Michigan Technological University who came to us as a consultant under that grant. Most notably I wish to thank Bill McKim, Director of the grant and Chair of the Literature and Language Department; Fran Zaniello, Co-Director of the grant and Director of the Writing Center; Peter Schiff, Coordinator of Teacher Training; Professors Sally Jacobsen and Susan Kissel in English; Professor Mary Carol Moses in Anthropology; and Professor Gary Johnston in Music. I am also grateful to Provost Lyle Gray and Northern Kentucky University for the Faculty Summer Fellowship which originally allowed me to pursue this research.

Judith Bechtel

*Improving Writing
and Learning*

1

Rationale

Writing is a process practiced by all educated people regardless of the area of their expertise. In spite of telephones, televisions, and computers, our society is still print-dominated. And for good reasons: writing is our most accessible way of making known what we are doing, and is also our oldest and most reliable method of learning.

In fact, the similarities between writing and learning are quite striking.[1] Both are active processes which utilize the whole brain, integrating sensory perceptions, experience, and memory on several levels simultaneously. Because writing is external and graphic, unlike speech, it can be deliberately reworked and improved in harmony with each person's individual work habits. Therefore, the people who can and do write well have the means of discovering knowledge and of knowing that they know—powerful advantages in an era when information becomes obsolete rapidly and career changes are regularly expected.

Writing skills are important for employability and promotion. The same skills also help synthesize observations, organize personality, and establish a constructive self-concept. In short, writing is central to the fullest attainment of human potential.

Why then has the development of writing ability been so largely ignored? Until recently writing ability had been assumed. And when, for various reasons, verbal skills could no longer be assumed, all attention riveted to reading deficiencies. Since reading is the primary mode of conveying academic information, a whole industry grew up in response to perceived deficiencies in reading. Researchers studied the reading process, teachers' colleges trained reading specialists, and textbook businesses promoted innumerable materials for developmental reading programs. Most public schools now have reading specialists on their staffs; many have reading laboratories. Ultimately books on reading were addressed to content teachers, urging them to teach reading in their classrooms.[2]

THE NEED FOR WRITING INSTRUCTION

Recent declines in the verbal abilities of high school and college students, well documented and variously explained in response to declining SAT (Scholastic Aptitude Test) scores, point to language difficulties other than reading problems. Quite obviously equal attention needs to be paid to careful instruction in writing if significant changes in performance are to be effected.

There are signs that such a movement is gearing up. Teachers' colleges are expecting their graduates to demonstrate writing competency, if not commitment to writing in the classroom. Universities are initiating workshops for faculty interested in incorporating writing into their course plans. And research into the process of writing is finally at the stage where wider dissemination of what is known can be useful to specialists outside the field of linguistics.

We know that no one develops writing skill without experience and practice. We also know that maturity in writing occurs when listening and speaking skills are encouraged concurrently. Wide reading is another necessary, but not sufficient, contributing experience to the development of writing. Through reading one becomes familiar with the sentence patterns, level of diction, and spelling that make later, more systematized study of language understandable. The so-called "back-to-basics" movement is thus somewhat misdirected when it is presumed that mastery of spelling and punctuation rules should precede productivity. It is the act of writing—giving external shape to what might be said about a topic—that teaches writing. There is no substitute for writing all along the way and not just as a "culminating experience."

Therefore, the teaching of writing, like the teaching of reading, has finally become everybody's business.

WHY WRITING INSTRUCTION IS RESISTED

There are many reasons why writing has not received the attention it deserves in content classrooms. In the first place, grading pieces of writing takes time, certainly much more time than scoring objective tests. With large classloads and competing pressures for use of professional time, few teachers feel they can afford the extra effort that writing assignments demand. Secondly, those who have assigned essay questions or outside reports have sometimes been so discouraged by their students' underdeveloped writing abilities that they have found it difficult to distinguish where knowledge of writing leaves off and knowledge of the content starts. Feeling inadequate to separate the two, content teachers frequently chose to isolate content learning to the "purest state"—the objective measurement of incremental data. The third factor influencing content teachers to minimize writing is the notion that English instruction is somebody else's job. Furthermore, most content teachers are convinced that they have no class time to devote to writing instruction; there is simply too much material to cover! Coupled with these notions of territorial prerogatives may be yet another cause for avoiding writing assignments; the content teachers' feelings of inadequacy about their own writing skill.

Each of these concerns is a legitimate, yet inadequate, rationalization for avoiding writing tasks. Although evaluation of writing tasks is time-consuming, there are ways to minimize that effort and to make it more efficient. For one thing, not all writing done needs to be evaluated. The careful design of an assignment and a limited focus of response will go a long way toward making time spent on assignments more efficient. Since students become involved with the subject matter through writing, the rewards of incorporating writing into a course plan are well worth the effort.

THE PAYOFFS FOR TEACHING WRITING

The fact that poor writing has discouraged some teachers from assigning writing is all the more reason why there is now a renewed interest in encouraging it. More is at stake than bad spelling or incorrect punctuation. When students are not given the experience of expressing relationships inherent in what they are studying, they lose the most valuable mode of discovering those relationships. In fact, they miss out on writing as a way of learning content. Furthermore, their notion that writing is not very important is reinforced. Some techniques for assessing ability level and designing appropriate assignments will go a long way toward encouraging students to develop their writing ability— and their understanding of what they are studying.

Still another reason to bring writing back into content classes is to eliminate some of the cheating that is now so widespread. Objective tests encourage dishonesty whereas essay tests have to be constructed privately. Term papers done outside of class also encourage cheating, as the open solicitation by ghost-writer term paper companies should make obvious. One reason that students copy rather than compose is that they simply don't know how to assimilate outside sources into their own writing. Plagiarism could be greatly reduced through careful attention to the design of research projects.

Teaching writing might be seen as the English teacher's responsibility, and indeed it is. The problem is that the English lessons must be practiced. If writing is not useful in other courses, students are not motivated to work on it even in English class. Also, the conventions of communication vary somewhat from subject to subject so that content teachers are best able to translate the principles of good writing into the particular conventions and thought patterns of their own discipline. Therefore, it is important for content teachers to be conscious of the various stages of the writing process and the differences between serious and superficial problems so that they can adapt what is taught in English class to the particular demands of their own discipline.

In all of this, content teachers need not apologize for their lack of familiarity with the terminology of grammar or even for their private worries about writing accurately. True, many content teachers may have chosen their field in part because it did not entail such demands on writing ability as some other specialties did. In fact, fear of writing even among language arts teachers is much more widespread than most teachers realize.[3] Some observers say that a premature and exaggerated preoccupation with accuracy is partly responsible for this fear.[4] At any rate, fear (of ridicule, of making mistakes?) is communicated from teachers to students and is one more factor in the avoidance of writing. Perhaps we have become slaves to a demand for perfection in writing that is unexpected in other endeavors. A more realistic view of the risks and pleasures of writing might encourage both students and teachers to do more of it.

THE CHALLENGE OF TEACHING WRITING

There are good reasons why writing ability is not easily taught and not easily learned. First, writing is a process and not a body of information. Therefore, you can't learn "about" writing the way you can about geography or biology. You just have to do it—over and over again. And the worst of it is that writing, unlike mathematical computing or tuning motors or other active processes, carries a unique emotional load. Writing is very closely associated with personality, with values, with intelligence. Criticism of writing thus becomes personal, no matter how carefully such criticism is couched in neutral or even supportive tones. Furthermore, our society as a whole, in spite of its print-domination, conveys very mixed cultural attitudes toward writing. The intellectual is mistrusted in America. Popular culture abounds in caricatures of the person who writes but can't relate. Working class or first-generation or nontraditional students (and increasingly these are the students we face) are particularly suspicious of writing and all that it represents. In addition, there are the unpleasant punishments associated with writing perpetuated by tradition: e.g., writing 100 times "I will not talk in class."

As if all of this were not enough of a current to swim against, there is a common-sense, man-in-the-street phenomenon associated with writing instruction. Almost everybody has a theory about what should be done with writing instruction. This is paradoxical, given the acknowledgement that "English is not their field" or that their own writing ability is not what they wish it were, but it seems that almost everybody has "an ax to grind" when it comes to writing. Part of the reason for this paradox is that everybody has had some experience with writing, some writing instruction. Often the emotional quality of this experience is what is retained and passed along. Then, too, the experts (English teachers and researchers) are in some disagreement, the specialty of writing instruction being so new in contrast to literary studies that have dominated the discipline for several centuries. All of this makes discussing writing a potentially volatile issue, compounded by differences over terminology, emphasis, and philosophy. Defensiveness steps in where prejudices seem to be undermined.

THE ASSUMPTIONS UNDERLYING THIS BOOK

It is with considerable jeopardy that any writing expert assumes an instructive stance. Therefore, it is more in the spirit of openness than of advocacy that the following assumptions about writing are presented. Each is explained more fully in subsequent chapters.

- Writing is a process that is central to learning. The writing process carries with it more emotional overtones than any other educational strategy.
- Writing is central to learning because of its usefulness for academic success and employability, and also because of the innate satisfactions related to discovering and controlling ideas.
- Writing instruction should exploit the full range of writing purposes: to aid memory by maintaining external records, to save readers time by reporting special knowledge, to affect action by convincing argument, to delight both writer and reader aesthetically.
- Learning to write is not an incremental process like learning calculus. Because verbal processing is associational as well as linear, a writer can return to earlier tasks with an ever-increasing, wider range of associations and hence a more mature performance.
- We cannot assume that the place to start writing instruction is with spelling or punctuation just because these are the first features noticed by a reader. Indeed, there is evidence that skill in editing comes late in the learning process and must be preceded by considerable experience in producing writing and in reading.

- The production of writing is not done in a linear sequence. One does not always have an idea and then put it into words. One often discovers meaning in the middle of the writing task. Incubation and rumination are factors here. Creating and editing must be seen as separate components of the writing process, each requiring its own mind set.
- Good writing assignments grow out of a total communication context. They are more than simply occasions to show off or to practice. The implied audience, the purpose of the writing, the role assumed by the writer must all be considered by the teacher when designing the assignment.
- The incorporation of writing into a content course is not just an extra feature or an added task. Good writing assignments grow out of a total theory of learning.
- How a piece of writing is responded to is of importance not only in judging it, but also in what is learned by it. How a piece will be responded to or evaluated is an integral part of how it is designed to fit into the course. Most teachers are not aware of their options in this regard.
- Although the principles of good writing can be more or less generally agreed upon across disciplines, the particular emphasis different features are given varies from discipline to discipline. It is up to content teachers to adopt those aspects of writing tasks which best suit their discipline and their philosophy of teaching.
- It is possible to distinguish between essential and irrelevant components of the writing process, between serious and superficial errors, between inexperienced and careless writers, between problems best left to the writing specialist and tasks appropriate for instruction in the content classroom.
- Writing is hard work and risky business, but it can only be done well by consistent practice. The satisfactions of writing outweigh the negative aspects for both student and teacher, however, and the best possible way of stressing its importance to the educational process is for every teacher to assume some responsibility for writing instruction. When content courses include few or no writing experiences, an indirect message about writing is conveyed: writing is not important.

Each of the above assumptions underlies the specific suggestions offered in succeeding chapters. Although the suggestions are very specific, they can be adapted for use in different subjects and at different levels of instruction. Most of the activities are appropriate for average high school students, making them easily adaptable to introductory college courses as well, especially when a high proportion of the students are from a different age bracket, social stratum, or educational background than their teachers are used to working with.

AN OVERVIEW OF THE BOOK

A direct knowledge of rhetoric and composition theory is not necessary for teachers interested in incorporating more writing into their class designs. For that reason, the focus of this book is on the practical, on what can be adapted from theory to fit the major needs of the classroom teacher.

The term "writing" refers to the selection and encoding of rhetorical units longer than one sentence. Implied is some degree of choice for the writer as to word selection, sentence structure, and even content. Discrimination among alternative possible responses and selection from among them is part of the writing process. In that sense all writing is creative or inventive; it is different from the mere recognition or manipulation of "givens" required for most objective tests. As such, writing covers a wide range of behaviors from taking notes to constructing poems.

Preliminary to designing writing assignments for students, the teacher must have a basic understanding of what writing entails and an estimate of the abilities and attitudes of the students. Most experienced teachers have reliable intuitions about these. But for teachers just beginning to think about the implications of writing for their courses or for teachers who have been disappointed in their earlier experiences with writing assignments, the place to start is with some goals in mind and with an assessment of the students' writing abilities in relation to these goals.

Chapter 2 describes more fully the theoretical base underlying writing across the curriculum, explaining the kind of frequent informal tasks that are at the heart of a comprehensive writing program. Only when students in all subjects are accustomed to freely writing their thoughts, indeed accustomed to arriving at thoughts *because* of writing them down, can they hope to complete the more complex tasks usually associated with academic writing.

Chapter 3 explains why assessment cannot be just a matter of interpreting standard test scores. The relationship between learning styles and specific content areas is explored as a preliminary step to designing assessment procedures. The interconnectedness of writing ability with reading ability and study skills is also explored. In many ways the selection of assessment instruments depends on the kinds of writing which will be required of the student.

Succeeding chapters offer examples of the range of writing assignments which could be built into the course structure. First come record-keeping tasks, those assignments which correlate most closely with reading instruction and the development of study skills. The range here is from notetaking to questioning and valuing sheets which become the basis of in-class discussions and brainstorming sessions.

All of these record-keeping tasks stress careful, directed reading and listening.

After basic record-keeping tasks come activities which integrate, synthesize, and translate materials into new or reorganized forms. These tasks are the most important for promoting understanding of the characteristic concepts of each discipline. Hence they are the most content-specific of the suggestions offered. The high order of manipulation called forth by these tasks requires that they build on the literal understanding of the content material. Yet these tasks, easily individualized to meet varying skill levels within a class, are clearly enjoyable because they allow for surprises and discoveries.

The chapter on research papers also covers ideas for unusual reports and creative research projects. Research papers or reports of one kind or another have always been and remain the most popular of writing assignments on the secondary level. The reason for this is that research papers, when correctly done, represent a sort of paradigm for the academic experience. Theoretically, they start with curiosity, proceed through discovering what has already been written about a topic, and then interpreting that data in relation to a hypothesis or central idea held by the writer. The problem is that research papers are rarely correctly done. Somehow preoccupation with the format of the report has pre-empted all interest in the research process involved in writing it. One difficulty is the complexity of the task, and the novice writer's inability to manage all of the component parts. Another difficulty is the basic irrelevance of the pursuit to the rest of the learning that is done in a particular course. For whatever reasons, the research paper is probably the most dreaded of all writing assignments, both by students who must write them and by teachers who must grade them. Careful preparation and follow-through of any writing task involving use of outside sources is a necessity. The chapter on research papers tells how and why.

No book on writing would be complete without some advice on constructing essay tests. The chapter on essay tests includes sample questions from several disciplines and also some hints about what to look for in evaluating answers. Included are categories of questions or topics which illustrate levels of involvement with the subject matter according to Bloom's taxonomy,[5] drawing careful attention to the choice of words used in giving directions for exams. A special feature of this chapter is the discussion of misunderstandings inherent in the essay test situation whereby students and teachers interpret the directions egocentrically. Attention is given to class activities and earlier writing tasks which help inexperienced students prepare for essay tests.

For those teachers who are willing to "go above and beyond the call of duty," there is a discussion of the value of creative writing in the content classroom. British educators do considerably more with this approach than we do in America.[6] This is true partially because we have considered creative writing to be private, subjective, and hence both uncriticizable and useless. None of these contentions is completely true, and there is really no solid reason—aside from tradition—that journals and poems could not be incorporated into the content classroom in tandem with factual reports. The chapter on creative writing offers some ways of stimulating and rewarding such efforts without compromising a basic commitment to standards and seriousness. In fact, these creative options often enhance cognitive development.

Although each chapter contains implicit directions for responding to the tasks described, the culminating chapter of the book discusses in detail what teachers' options are in responding to student writing. More has been written on evaluation than on any other single aspect of classroom writing. Therefore, this chapter is a full one, beginning with an overview of the effect of teacher response on student learning. Several ways of responding to student writing are described in detail, depending on whether a piece of writing represents an early draft or a finished paper. Nonjudgmental questions, instead of corrections or grades, are appropriate responses to informal class writing. Peer evaluation is also recommended for in-process papers. On the other hand, primary trait checklists might be an efficient and fair way to grade finished research papers. In all cases the response methods must match the purpose of the assignment.

Since many teachers are unaware of the many options open to them in responding to student writing, several different methods are described in detail. Sometimes several of these methods can be combined to turn the writing project into an integral part of the coursework and information sharing which happens during the class. Throughout the chapter on evaluation, there is an implicit distinction between evaluation procedures which judge (as in placement tests and exit exams) and response procedures which teach.

This book is intended not so much as a "cookbook" as an "appetite whetter" whereby innovative teachers will be inspired to concoct their own writing assignments, perhaps quite different from any of the specific suggestions made here. The point is that there are "many roads to Mecca." For writing assignments to be right assignments for you, they must seem relevant and interesting. You must feel committed enough to want to spend the time working on them, since writing certainly does take time.

One way to discover whether your writing assignments are good ones is to do them yourself. If you learn from the experience, chances are that your students will, too.

NOTES

1. For a fuller explanation see Janet Emig, "Writing as a Mode of Learning," *College Composition and Communication* 28 (May 1977): 122–128.

2. See, for example, Robert C. Aukerman, *Reading in the Secondary Classroom* (New York: McGraw-Hill Book Co., 1972); Emerald Dechant, *Reading Improvement in the Secondary School* (Englewood Cliffs, NJ: Prentice-Hall, Inc., 1964); Thomas H. Estes and Joseph L. Vaughan, Jr., *Reading and Learning in the Content Classroom* (Boston: Allyn and Bacon, Inc., 1978); Robert Karlin, *Teaching Reading in High School* (Indianapolis, Indiana: Bobbs-Merrill Co., 1972); H.A. Robinson and Lamar Thomas, *Improving Reading in Every Class* (Boston: Allyn and Bacon, 1973); and David L. Shepherd, *Comprehensive High School Reading Methods* (Columbus, Ohio: Charles E. Merrill Publishing Company, 1973).

3. John L. Daly has made extensive studies of writing apprehension. See, for example, his "Writing Apprehension in the Classroom: Teacher Role Expectations of the Apprehensive Writer," *Research in the Teaching of English* 13 (February 1979): 37–44.

4. Representative of these observers is Donald J. Lloyd, "Our National Mania for Correctness," *The American Scholar* 21 (Summer 1952): 283–289.

5. B.S. Bloom, Ed., *Taxonomy of Educational Objectives: Handbook I, Cognitive Domain* (New York: David McKay Co., 1956).

6. See, for example, Arthur H. Applebee, "Writing Across the Curriculum: The London Projects," *English Journal* 66 (December 1977): 81–88.

2

A New View of Writing

Just what is meant by "writing across the curriculum"? Surely we want to improve student writing, but that is actually only a by-product of writing across the curriculum. The main thrust is using writing to learn the information and concepts of a content course. The idea of writing to learn (instead of writing to communicate what *has* already been learned) is at once so obvious and so revolutionary that teachers will wonder why it has received so little attention.

FORMER ASSUMPTIONS

Formerly writing in content courses was assumed to mean learning the forms and style of the professional writing in that discipline, or at least learning the forms and style of academic discourse in general. For example, science students learned to write laboratory reports, and students in all courses learned to write research papers. Those tasks are still appropriate, but they are by no means the starting point of writing across the curriculum.

Formerly it was assumed that to teach writing in a given subject, the teacher had to know all about writing and all about the content area. We now know that neither of these specialties is mandatory. An English teacher who is relatively unfamiliar with biology or U.S. government can learn (and write) along with students under the guidance of a content teacher in introductory content courses, and in that sharing serve as a model of a person writing in order to learn. On the other hand, a content teacher who has had no special training in writing can encourage more of it by simply considering writing in a new way.

EXPRESSIVE WRITING

At the heart of writing across the curriculum is the idea of frequent, but short informal writing. Such writing is more or less like "thoughts or inner speech" written down because it is natural-sounding, speculative, and rambling. Apparently such notes to oneself, although largely ignored in assigned schoolwork, are natural precursors to the more organized and formal writing we normally associate with schoolwork. The British call it "expressive" writing, meaning writing which *expresses* what one is considering rather than *communicates* what one is sure of.[1]

Whenever new experiences or new information are introduced —whether in lectures, from reading, or through direct experience— students are invited to respond in writing with summaries, associations, questions, or comments. These written responses are used in various ways, sometimes as the beginnings of more polished papers, sometimes as springboards for further discussion. The important thing about expressive writing is that it is never marked for errors, and it is never graded (although it may be "counted"). The only appropriate response to this kind of writing is supportive concern for the content and ideas expressed, usually by writing context-specific comments or questions in the margins or at the end.

The lack of correction does not mean, however, that accuracy is not important in writing across the curriculum; only that these informal, focused, expressive writings should not cause students to worry about the conventions of formal writing. Without trust students will not feel free to write what is really on their minds, and learning by writing will not occur. Fear of making mistakes can and does inhibit fluency.

The point of expressive writing is to build the habit of writing, of using pen and paper as an external, deliberate aid to thinking. Many students are completely alienated from their own best writing processes, and particularly the earlier, speculative stages of thinking before firm concepts have taken shape.[2] Such students are preoccupied with the judgmental, punitive aspects of writing, having never experienced the freedom or pleasures of making discoveries through writing. Most teachers, on the other hand, have internalized the processes of critical thinking and are more or less able to express coherent and well-formed ideas directly onto paper. Therefore, the notion of using writing in a tentative and uncensored way seems strange and unnecessary to many students and to many teachers. Yet it is quite possible that significant learning occurs only if and when students adopt a speculative frame of mind, allowing themselves to make connections between what is new to them and what they already know.

Such writing is more than a rehearsal of facts; it involves the selection of those facts which either harmonize or clash with past learning. Such writing is the opposite of mere verbalism, and it is full of surprises. A student from Kentucky, familiar with the cities in his own state, may be completely baffled upon hearing that the Revolutionary War soldiers traveled from Concord to Lexington; he is thinking that this means they traveled from New England to central Kentucky![3] Another student of social studies, upon hearing how dense the population is in Japan, surmises that Japanese people are small because they all must fit into so small a land.[4] Such connections—whether appropriate or inappropriate—are made all the time by active learners. But without regular writing they are often buried beneath the level of conscious attention. Expressive writing can bring out these connections, thus serving as the cutting edge of learning.

THE PURPOSES OF EXPRESSIVE WRITING

The necessity of recasting things into one's own words rather than immediately into the forms traditional to specific disciplines (such as formal lab reports) cannot be overemphasized. British researchers even go so far as to say:

> It is in the child's own vernacular speech, which is often very far away from standard, that he's at his most powerful, the most comfortable; this is where all his richest meanings lie.[5]

This starting point is what is encouraged as "a student's right to his own language,"[6] the idea being that a person's speech patterns are integrally tied to the inner speech of thought. To allow thoughts to be expressed as they are experienced is to accept a person's inner reality. To disallow a person's inner speech patterns by insisting on such regularities as standard verb forms is to cut that person off from his or her own honest responses.

An active learner is always pushing beyond specific information toward a more generalized framework to hang it on. By going beyond the given data, a student forms abstractions. Even the audience and referent become abstractions in writing whereas they are present and concrete in conversation. If science students are discussing their sketches of the movement of glaciers, they can point to their sketches and tell immediately from the looks on their peers' faces whether or not what they are saying is being accepted. But what they write about glacial movement will have to stand alone, without sketches, without gestures, without the immediate context of the activity. Thus even informal writing introduces the abstracting of audience and purpose.

Furthermore, the act of writing itself generates new thoughts by calling up associations. Writing about glaciers, for example, may cause new realizations about glacial movement. Pursuing her notion that glacial movement is something like river movement, a student realizes that friction against bedrock accounts for the fact that a glacier moves more at its top and center than at its bottom or sides. Without expressive writing, this student would have been content to remember that glaciers move unevenly.

Students in English classes should also be encouraged to explore their initial reactions to pieces of literature through short informal writing that resembles talk written down. They should be encouraged to express dislike or admiration for characters in stories, for instance, without regard to the terminology of literary criticism. These initial responses may be idiosyncratic or even misguided, but such gropings are a necessary and exciting first step toward mature interpretations. To make no provision for such exploration of personal reactions is to encourage only superficial engagement with literature.[7]

Several factors seem to contribute to such leaps from data to insight. One factor is new material or tasks slightly beyond the student's past experience that make writing almost a necessity for making sense of the material. Another factor is a strong emotional component, such as shock or surprise, to the material or in the situation surrounding its presentation. Good teachers seem intuitively to exploit these opportunities, but expressive writing enhances them. And when students are pushed beyond their initial (often superficial) responses, through questioning or simply through requests for longer pieces of writing, they often surprise themselves with new insights. A record of these insights can and should lead students to recognize and celebrate what they know. Knowing that they know is yet another important, though neglected, aspect of learning.

THE ADVANTAGES OF WRITING OVER TALK

Short informal responses to new material are more than first steps toward more sophisticated writing. In responding immediately and freely to new information, students are actively integrating the material with what they already know, and they are paying better attention while they read or listen. The physical act of writing also reinforces memory. Of course, many of these functions also occur during good class discussions. Talk and verbal questioning are important in understanding new material. But passive students can easily remain silent during class discussions, leaving all the active involvement to their more vocal peers. Also, the first few contributions made during a class discussion set the tenor of the whole discussion, leaving unexamined other problems or interpretations which never get considered. These unexamined topics would have been recorded if writing had been encouraged prior to the discussion.

THE UNCOMFORTABLE TRUTH

One inevitable outcome of encouraging informal or expressive writing is that teachers find out more than they really want to know. Teachers may feel discouraged about the blatant misunderstandings or inflexible attitudes which are often expressed in these informal writings. The thing to remember, however, is that these problems were there all along; it is just that writing calls them to the surface of our students' and our own awarenesses. Then they can be dealt with or responded to by the teacher, either directly or indirectly. Sometimes the teacher's response is to present information in an entirely different way the next time.

In fact, it is fair to say that the introduction of frequent expressive writing eventually affects every other aspect of course design, from the presentation of material to the evaluation of student accomplishment. Although many content teachers begin with the idea of merely adding some writing to the other things they already do, the "added on" writing soon causes other realignments by revealing gaps or cognitive misunderstandings. Most often this triggers a reassessment of that old standby, the lecture. Teachers realize that "covering" the material is somewhat of an illusion, referring to what has been given, not what has been received. Besides, certain attitudes and skills cannot be conveyed through lectures. And even when the subject matter is appropriate to a lecture format, the same lecture may be boring to the able student but too fast for the less able. Still, the lecture remains the most efficient and time-honored mode of conveying information, and using writing in conjunction with it cannot help but enhance receptivity.

HOW TO BUILD ON EXPRESSIVE WRITING

Using short, regular, informal writing as the centerpiece of any course does not mean that only this kind of writing will be encouraged. From there students can go in either of two directions with their writing: toward straight "academic" prose or toward more artistic, poetic writing. James Britton called academic prose "transactional" writing, meaning writing intended to transact business, to convey information, to persuade, or to get a reader to respond in a particular way.[8] Of course, most school writing is transactional writing. To the possible detriment of many learners' fullest development, students have few opportunities to develop the associational and metaphorical powers of understanding inherent in artistic, poetic writing. The point here, however, is not really to expand on the differences between writing styles, but to suggest that *all* public writing—whether transactional or poetic—derives from the same private source, expressive writing.

Given the information that can be presented in any course, and given the variety of writing tasks which can be assigned, teachers might want to use expressive writing as the crucial link in student learning. The ways short focused writing could serve this linking function are numerous:

- *Journals.* Students can keep journals or learning logs, making regular entries after readings or midway through lectures. These journals, collected periodically, become the basis of discussions and

FIGURE 2.1

INFORMAL WRITING AS THE SOURCE OF ALL PUBLIC WRITING

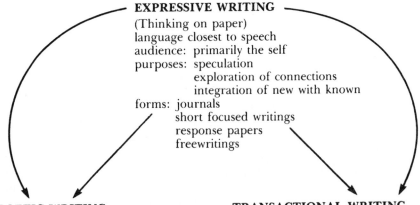

EXPRESSIVE WRITING
(Thinking on paper)
language closest to speech
audience: primarily the self
purposes: speculation
　　　　　exploration of connections
　　　　　integration of new with known
forms: journals
　　　　short focused writings
　　　　response papers
　　　　freewritings

POETIC WRITING
(Constructs)
self-conscious manipulation of
　language conventions
audience: other private individuals
purposes: shape experience
　　　　　delight and entertain
　　　　　share insight
forms: essays
　　　　poems
　　　　stories

TRANSACTIONAL WRITING
(Academic and commercial prose)
standard English used
audience: scholars and professionals
purposes: explanation
　　　　　persuasion
forms: reports
　　　　letters
　　　　term papers
　　　　tests

Source: Adapted from James Britton, Tony Burgess, Nancy Martin, Alex McLeod, and Harold Rosen. *The Development of Writing Abilities (11–18).* London: Macmillan Education, Ltd., 1975. © Schools Council Publications 1975 and Macmillan, London and Basingstoke.

other class activities. They also influence later explanation and presentations in class.

- *Public class journals.* Students can contribute a page a week to a public class journal available to all. Students can read each other's thoughts and write down comments or questions in response to them. The results are increased involvement and an ever-widening sense of audience.
- *Free-writings.* Free-writings are simply timed writings that encourage fluency. The idea is to free-associate and ramble rather than plan and plod. Quantity rather than quality is encouraged. It soon develops, however, that it is almost impossible to write nonsense; that the subconscious mind creates its own order; that the experience of writing "faster" than you can think becomes refreshing. Free-writings often generate good insights.
- *Ditto pages to share.* Expressive writing can be done directly on ditto as homework assignments to be duplicated and read by the whole class. The necessity of writing something down, but the freedom to do so informally, offers students the chance to commit themselves to something prior to a lecture or class discussion. As such, this task can substitute for a study guide or quiz while at the same time serving as a discussion primer.

Figure 2.2 suggests the importance of expressive writing for integrating what the students think with what is presented in class and what may be possible to do in more complex writing tasks. More ideas for building other assignments around expressive writing are presented in each chapter of this book.

One challenge for the content teacher is to set up sequences whereby expressive writing helps students prepare for more complex tasks. Ironically, expressive writing itself makes teachers aware of these kinds of strategies. For example, from a batch of social studies writings interpreting various charts about world population and hunger, one teacher became aware that students could not interpret charts. Practice with making and interpreting charts had to precede the writing of formal reports in that class.

PUTTING "GRAMMAR" IN ITS PLACE

For teachers worried about how matters of organization and mechanical accuracy will be learned if they are not insisted upon in every piece of writing, we have the assurance of many experts that these are considerations for later attention. This means later in two senses: later in the production of any particular piece of writing and later in the student's life. In fact, if the British experience is any indication, gross

FIGURE 2.2

EXPRESSIVE WRITING: THE ALL-IMPORTANT LINK

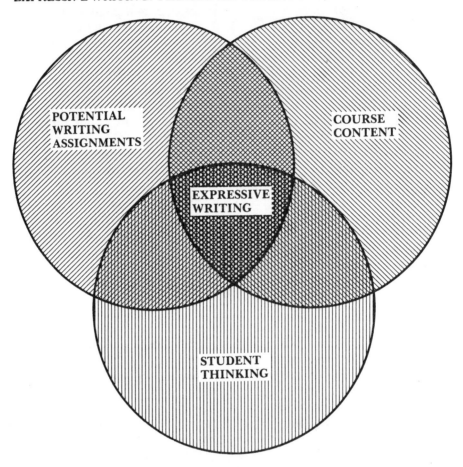

problems in sentence structure and spelling would be rare among adolescent writers if all teachers in all subjects in all grades encouraged the kind of writing described here.

An intuitive grasp of regularities cannot be taught directly. It must be closely tied to aesthetic perceptions and comes only with guided experience in speaking, listening, reading, and writing.[9] James Britton puts it this way:

> There's a lot of evidence that although the study of the structure of language is a fascinating study, it's not a way of improving your control over language. But the other things, like using the acceptable forms of punctuation and spelling—these are abilities picked up in the course of *using* writing, and effectively picked up if you care

about your writing, and you care about your writing if you are getting some satisfaction from it, and you're getting some satisfaction from it if it's pursuing your own purpose and not simply toeing the line of somebody else's purposes.[10]

By focusing on the place where writing and thinking come together, content teachers can contribute to their students' total cognitive development while yet guiding their acquisition of the content material. The improvement of writing ability is secondary, caused mainly by stressing the naturalness of the act of writing. In that sense, time spent on writing is really "back to the basics"—the basics of study skills, the basics of self-concept, and the basics of learning new information pertaining to a subject area.

Content teachers have realized all along that it was too much to ask them to teach the mechanics of writing in addition to all else they were expected to do. Now they have an alternative to taking writing ability for granted or not expecting their students ever to write at all.

A NEW CONCEPTION OF WRITING

We have too long held writing up on a pedestal. We have thought of it with awe—all those rules of grammar, correct spelling, twenty-page term.papers, and so forth. We tend to think of writing as a finished product to be judged by demanding, absolute standards.

Certainly these expectations hold true for most transactional writing, both academic and commercial. Teaching the skills to do these tasks well should still be our program's ultimate goal. But by limiting ourselves to this notion of what writing is, we have inadvertently cut students off from the possibility of achieving it. Granted, we want students eventually to write mature academic prose. It does not follow, however, that we should give them practice only with those forms. Requiring traditional research papers and essays at younger and younger ages does not necessarily prepare students to do them well. Some theorists have even suggested that abstract thinking (which is required for most academic prose) does not usually develop prior to the late high school years.[11] Overemphasizing the forms of academic prose without the requisite understanding merely promotes boredom.

When students are asked to generate material they do not really understand, they write empty verbalisms that "sound" like what has been requested but do not reflect commitment or thought. Why? Because, for one thing, many students are simply inexperienced with critical thinking and with writing, both of which are inextricably intertwined. Not conscious of or familiar with the sub-processes of complex writing tasks, many students will simply get the assignment done in the quickest, least painful way.

Another problem with the usual expectations regarding school writing concerns the artificiality of communication when the writer must explain something to a reader who knows more about it than the writer does. It should be obvious that school writing is often a perversion of the normal communication situation where the writer knows more and must, therefore, share with or explain to a relatively uninformed reader. Under normal school conditions, on the other hand, the reader (the teacher) is actually more of an examiner. Not surprisingly, when the reader has this limited role of examiner, the writer experiences an equally narrow sense of purpose: to pass the examination. With expressive writing, students write for themselves or their peers rather than for an examiner. They write with the intention of raising questions or posing hypothetical situations.

Expressive writing on a regular basis as an integral part of course design will not replace the need for more polished prose to be judged and evaluated; it just sets the stage for such a possibility. It takes finished, polished prose out of a vacuum.

Traditional writing assignments often ignore the writing process. By giving directions which merely describe the traits expected in a finished paper (everything from its length to the number of errors allowable), teachers offer little guidance to students about *how* to proceed. Neither traditional directions nor traditional evaluation procedures take into consideration *how* a person writes. Some students seem to know how to proceed, others obviously have difficulties, and this discrepancy contributes to the widespread notion that writing can't be taught, that some people just have a "talent" for it. Allowing for differences in ability and granting the special inspiration required for Belle Lettres, we now know that all writers, no matter what the task, do follow more or less predictable procedures, some more efficiently than others, when they write. When assignments enhance these procedures, rather than ignore them, students learn better how to write.

THE WRITING PROCESS

It seems evident, then, that expressive writing, the centerpiece of writing across the curriculum, is really only a first step toward mature writing. Its appeal lies in its simplicity, the removal of certain constraints such as attention to organization or punctuation. Normally writing entails the manipulation of so many complex, interlocking strategies that they cannot all be attended to at once. There are social constraints: the writer's purpose and sense of what readers expect. There are psychological constraints: the writer's past experiences and values. There are graphemic constraints: the manual dexterity involved in forming letters. There are cognitive constraints: the selection and wording of the message. Some of these must be attended to automatically for writing to occur at all. Experienced writers do attend to most of these constraints automatically, calling up correct spellings, for example, without really being conscious of doing so. But for inexperienced writers to tackle complex tasks, some allowance has to be made for the limited repertoire of automatic processes they can count on. They need to be made more aware of processes that more experienced writers take for granted.

Teachers who keep journals or who write their own assignments are more likely to be aware of the writing process than those who are removed from the experience of writing, those whose closest dealing with writing comes from grading student papers. The experience of grading usually results in a list of desirable traits of a finished piece of writing. The experience of writing, though, makes us conscious of all the problems inherent in the process of writing, a summary of which is offered below.

Pre-writing

Once students get used to writing informally, they have learned a strategy useful in the preparation of longer, more formal papers; they will have learned a way of saying something. Stage I of the writing process, often called "pre-writing" (in this case, somewhat of a misnomer), is to come up with ideas *from which to choose* a topic or a special slant to take on a topic. Pre-writing occurs during lively discussions, but it is best encouraged through expressive writing, where it can be looked at and reworked later. Because writing is a recursive process (the steps are not neatly sequential, but move forward and circle back repeatedly), pre-writing or ideating may occur midway through a long writing project and not necessarily only before the project is begun, even though it is usually considered the first step.

Incubating

Before, during, and after pre-writing, ideas must incubate or take time to jell and form themselves in the brain. Incubation is the magical working of the subconscious mind that helps writers to make decisions and solve problems even when they are not consciously working on their writing. This stage of the writing process often is going on while a person is procrastinating, waiting until the last minute to complete an assignment. In fact, that is one reason why writing can often be done quicker at the last minute than if the process is systematically spread out over a longer time period. The incubation period often pays off, especially for more experienced writers. On the other hand, incubation is most effective when expressive writing has first been done, later to be transformed into more formal prose.

It is largely because of the new ideas that come from pre-writing and incubating that many writers cannot and should not begin a writing task by constructing an outline. Sometimes a pre-conceived plan, such as an outline, inhibits insights. Furthermore, outlines conceived before new material has been explored tend to be so superficial as to be useless. Of course, a finished piece of academic prose should be well organized and "outlinable," but writers and tasks differ as to when in the writing process this "jelling" should occur.

Writing an Initial First Draft

In theory, once something is down on paper, it is easier to organize and revise than while it is still just an idea or a problem in the mind. The trouble with most inexperienced writers, however, is that they don't distinguish between writing a first draft and revising or editing it. Instead, inexperienced writers, because of their teachers' concerns about correctness, often confuse the first-draft process with the later, more critical stages of the writing process. In short, they worry about spelling, punctuation, and sentence structure at the very time when they should be thinking about content, about what they mean to say. One of the most exhilarating experiences writers can have is the freedom to write quickly a rough first draft without concern for spelling or even for paragraphing. Instead, most inexperienced writers cramp up, too worried about editing to let their ideas flow.

There are many techniques for changing students' habits about first and only drafts. One is to encourage frequent inclass expressive writing, parts of which might be considered first drafts. Another is to encourage students to turn in rough drafts for suggestions from their peers on revision. If students get used to writing rough drafts on one side of the paper for later cutting and pasting, they will gain a sense of control over what they write.

Revising

Once first drafts are encouraged, revising loses its punitive sting. Revising is not a matter of making a final paper acceptable; it is a matter of giving shape to a paper *in process*. Revising means rearranging, changing emphasis, adding or deleting information. Sometimes the addition of introductions and conclusions is considered to be revising.

It is at this stage of the writing process that writers should be encouraged to outline as one means of gaining control over what they write. It is important for teachers not to be too directive at this stage. Otherwise revisions become not a matter of control, but instead a matter of "giving the teacher what he wants." Peers asking questions offer the best motivation for revising.

Editing

Once a paper is organized and revised, then comes the critical, judgmental part of the process: the eagle's eye catching words left out, mis-

---

FIGURE 2.3

THE WRITING PROCESS

INCUBATION ◄──────► PRE-WRITING
(thinking about the task, letting ideas jell)

PRE-WRITING
(finding a topic or slant on a topic, generating ideas, getting started, thinking on paper)
- interpretive notetaking
- class discussion
- lists and outlines
- questions
- class activities
- informal writing

FIRST DRAFTS
(rough or slop drafts)
- informal writing
- initial write-up of formal papers

REVISING
(rearrangements through additions, deletions, changes of emphasis in first drafts)
- conferences with peers or teacher
- reading piece aloud for own or others' reactions
- revision sheets for guided changes
- changes made after passage of time

EDITING
(proofreading, corrections of errors in sentence structure, punctuation, and spelling)
- reading piece aloud or from end to beginning
- marking errors spotted in someone else's writing
- editing sheets for guided changes

Source: Adapted from chart devised by Frances Zaniello, Director of The Writing Center, Northern Kentucky University.

spellings, missing punctuation, and so forth. Sometimes this process is easier for objective eyes than it is for writers to do with their own papers. Sometimes gimmicks like reading from the end of a paper to its beginning work as a means of focusing on mechanics while editing. At any rate, two things seem obvious about editing: 1) inexperienced writers, unused to the regularities, cannot edit well, and yet 2) once a paper is in shape otherwise, it is *very* easy for an experienced writer to make the superficial changes that would make it "correct."

Linguists have coined the term "surface-structure" to describe what we see on paper, which may contain careless errors or dialectical variations, as distinct from a person's intended meaning and basic knowledge of the language.[12] Any business person knows the value of a good secretary for correcting surface-structure errors. Yet it is amazing how much weight we place in academic writing on matters of superficial editing. In fact, teachers as graders often function as their students' editors. The point here is not that editing is unimportant; only that it is not the *most important* stage of the writing process.

Figure 2.3 illustrates the various stages of the writing process. In actuality, the process is not nearly so linear as it appears, or as it would seem to be logically. Writers apparently alternate between pre-writing, incubating, drafting, incubating some more, revising, editing, rereading what they have written, and so forth. Even a clear revising session involves some drafting, for example, since new material may be added during revisions. And each stage of the writing process requires a somewhat different frame of mind. The pre-writing must be relatively free-wheeling whereas the editing must be critical and judgmental.

THE EFFECTS OF DIRECTIONS AND GRADING ON PROCESS

Teachers can help students with the writing process, through the directions they give for writing assignments and in the way they grade those assignments. Yet teachers' comments on student papers more often than not reflect confusion about whether the student is at the beginning or near the end of the writing process. Listed below, for illustration, are a variety of comments which could very well have been written on the very same draft of a student paper. Notice that each one presupposes a different stage of the writing process.

- "You need more information about chromosomes." (This suggests the student is at the pre-writing stage, still coming up with information to include in the paper.)

FIGURE 2.4

CHECKLIST FOR A GOOD WRITING ASSIGNMENT

APPROPRIATE
Takes into account the age, maturity, ability, experience, and interests
of the writer
Relates to ideas and materials being used at the time or very recently   _____
Connects what has been learned in the past to what is to be or can be
learned in the future   _____

STIMULATING
Engages the writer in a controversy, a quest for an answer, or some
accurate observation that is worthwhile but not too personal   _____
Gives choices, offers options   _____

INSTRUCTIVE
Draws upon, or furnishes, adequate data   _____
Provides a controlling idea, either a proposition or a topic stated or
readily construable into a proposition, which the writer is to explain
or support   _____
Provides one or more cues for content   _____
Provides one or more cues for organization   _____
Specifies limits, conditions, and/or the expected performance   _____
Focuses on one writing skill that has been previously taught   _____
Encourages experimentation, original or critical thinking, a chance
to "fool around" with ideas or language or both   _____

PURPOSEFUL
Helps the writer use or find an appropriate voice or self   _____
Identifies or implies a real audience   _____
Enables discovery, a chance to use what has been learned—and learn
what can be used   _____

Source: Helen J. Throckmorton, "Do Your Writing Assignments Work?—Checklist for a Good
Writing Assignment," *English Journal* 69 (November 1980): 58. Copyright © 1980 by the National Council of Teachers of English. Reprinted by permission of the publisher and author.

FIGURE 2.5

CHECKLIST FOR GOOD DIRECTIONS ON WRITING ASSIGNMENTS
_____ 1. Directions written out and distributed to class.
_____ 2. Topic or range of topics, including limitations on possible slants to take
on topic, clearly specified.
_____ 3. Purpose (whether informative, persuasive, entertaining, etc.) mentioned.
_____ 4. Audience named, including any use the paper might be put to such as
being duplicated for future classes, being submitted for publication, etc.
_____ 5. Intellectual demands explained in ways that suggest appropriate procedures for students to follow in completing the assignment.
_____ 6. Evaluation criteria listed, including expectations about length, format,
level of formality, organization, submission of notes or first drafts, etc.—
if possible, including the checklist that may actually be used in grading
the assignment.

Source: Adapted from Anne J. Herrington, "Writing to Learn: Writing Across the Disciplines,"
College English 43 (April 1981): 379–387.

- "The second and third paragraphs should be reversed to create a more logical order." (This suggests the student is at the revising stage where rearrangements and changes of emphasis are attended to.)
- "You misspelled *Mendel*." (This suggests the student is at the editing stage, the final stage of the writing process, when matters of spelling and punctuation are checked.)

Each of these comments might be helpful to students, but not if they appear on the same draft or as comments on a finished paper.

Given the complexity of the writing process, students have to be powerfully motivated in order to expend the energy needed for prewriting, incubation, drafting, revising, and editing. They need to feel that the effort is worthwhile. They need to find the assignment appropriate, stimulating, instructive, and purposeful. These are all factors to consider in designing formal writing tasks. Figure 2.4 is a checklist which takes these factors into account.

Once the assignment is defined, however, the teacher needs to come up with helpful directions. These should always be given in writing to eliminate later misunderstandings. Each stage of the writing process should be accounted for, directly or indirectly. Ideally this means in-class time for expressive writing that will help students discover a particular slant on a topic or problem needing a solution. It also means early submission of first drafts for peer revision and editing. In general, good directions also specify a purpose and intended audience, some suggestions for proceeding, and the criteria by which the paper will be evaluated. Figure 2.5 is a checklist of what to include in good directions.

SMALL GROUP WORK

As more writing is introduced, the use of more and better talking-for-learning seems to be a natural feature of the classroom. Usually this means using small groups, a practice that has earned a bad name because it can be such a waste of time when the participants don't know what they are doing. In small groups students read each other their informal writings, question each other, and clarify misunderstandings. In the process new problems or solutions come to the fore that can be reported back to the whole class.

Most students and most teachers are not yet used to working in small groups. Yet if classes are carefully prepared for their small group work, and if the teacher is willing to relinquish occasional class time for this activity, student involvement with learning can be improved remarkably. Each subsequent chapter contains some suggestions for small group work.

Although informal writing can begin rather inconspicuously in the content classroom, the use of small groups is a noticeable change. This is particularly true during the adolescent years when many social constraints interfere with peer interaction. Discipline problems and general school atmosphere also contribute to the problems of using small groups. However, the rewards are usually worth the effort. One indirect reward is the sense of community that develops among students, a condition that some educators think must be established if good learning is to occur at all.[13]

HOW TO BEGIN SMALL GROUPS

Experienced teachers tell us to begin by announcing that small groups will be used later in the course, thus letting students get used to the idea first.[14] There must exist an atmosphere of trust for sharing writing. Students react to each other's writing the way their teachers have reacted to theirs, or they withhold participation altogether if not comfortable with the way they've seen their teachers react to writing. Some ways to build trust about the short focused writings are to avoid ridicule of mistakes, ask permission of any student whose writing you intend to share with the whole class, respond to papers with questions and information rather than corrections, and, above all, write with the students and share what you have written. These supportive responses can be offered deliberately a few at a time, spread over several weeks.

Eventually the class will become acclimated to the idea of collaborative learning, especially if they have had plenty of preparation, if they are allowed to form groups of their own choosing, and if they are given a very structured task the first time they work together. Some teachers have found that the best way to keep groups on task and supportive is to have them read their own papers aloud, then answer such generalized questions as: What part of the paper really communicated? What would you like to have heard more about? What suggestions do you have for making the paper better? Using small groups in this way is a natural outgrowth of encouraging expressive writing, a supplement to lectures, and a help to the teacher in responding to student writing. Small group work is almost always the next step after eliciting lots of writing.

WHERE SMALL GROUPS GO WRONG

Since groups are best at reflecting and problem-solving, these qualities also should be valued in the class tests. Students will view small groups as a waste if they don't learn from them skills that count. Too often teachers give the same quantitative tests after introducing teaching methods that go beyond recall of facts. A history test matching dates and battles would not seem to follow logically from a set of class activities which encouraged empathy for the value conflicts of the Civil War.

For teachers uncomfortable with giving up this much control or in situations where group work is impractical for other reasons, the short focused writing can still be of great use. Writing, even informal writing, can be part of the class homework assignments, and good talk will inevitably occur outside of class whenever stimulating learning is going on inside.

SUMMARY

The philosophy underlying writing across the curriculum is based on research. Specifically, research has shown us that learning to write is not sequential the way learning algebra is. As with acquiring oral language, learning to write occurs most naturally when the conscious focus of attention is on content. Therefore, sequential writing objectives are not nearly so valuable for stepping stones as the constant and school-wide use of thoughts-written-down. This is the best means of bridging the gap between present understanding and potential mastery of new material.

Writing across the curriculum means writing more often, writing more informally, and writing more openly than usual. It also means using writing as an integral part of the learning process, not merely as a test measure to determine what has already been learned. It means giving credit for doing some kinds of writing without correction or grading. And it means building other class activities around expressive writing.

Such writing may very well lead to the more complex formal assignments usually associated with particular disciplines, or it may lead to mastery of the style and form characteristic of all good academic writing. Conscious attention to the writing process should be part of the planning of these more complex assignments. How all of this can be achieved is more fully discussed in the chapters that follow.

NOTES

1. Adapted from James Britton, Tony Burgess, Nancy Martin, Alex McLeod, and Harold Rosen, *The Development of Writing Abilities (11–18)* (London: Macmillan Education, 1975).

2. See explanation in Randy Freisinger, "Cross Disciplinary Writing Workshops: Theory and Practice," *College English* 42 (October 1980): 154–166.

3. An experience recalled by Robert Gschwind, School Administrator, Fort Thomas, Kentucky.

4. An experience reported by Pat D'Arcy in "Writing Across the Disciplines," a workshop presented at the National Convention of the National Council of Teachers of English in Cincinnati, Ohio, November, 1980.

5. Harold Rosen quoted in Lois Rosen, "An Interview with James Britton, Tony Burgess, and Harold Rosen," *English Journal* 57 (November 1978): 52.

6. Policy statement issued by the National Council of Teachers of English at their 1973 National Convention.

7. For a fuller discussion of the reader-response method of approaching literature, see David Bleich, *Readings and Feelings: An Introduction to Subjective Criticism* (Urbana, Illinois: National Council of Teachers of English, 1975) or Louise Rosenblatt, *The Reader, the Text, the Poem* (Carbondale, Illinois: Southern Illinois University Press, 1978).

8. Britton et al, *The Development of Writing Abilities (11–18)*.

9. From William F. Irmscher, "Writing as a Way of Learning and Developing," *College Composition and Communication* 30 (October 1979): 240–244.

10. Quoted in Lois Rosen, "An Interview with James Britton, Tony Burgess, and Harold Rosen."

11. See, for example, Bärbel Inhelder and Jean Piaget, *The Early Growth of Logic in the Child* (New York: W.W. Norton and Co., 1969).

12. For an overview of linguistic concepts see Constance Weaver, *Grammar for Teachers: Perspectives and Definitions* (Urbana, Illinois: National Council of Teachers of English, 1978).

13. See, for example, William Pinar, Ed., *Curriculum Theorizing: The Reconceptualists* (Berkeley, California: McCutcheon Publishers, 1975).

14. See, for example, Mary K. Healy, *Using Student Writing Response Groups in the Classroom* (Berkeley, California: Bay Area Writing Pamphlet No. 12, 1980).

3

Assessment of Student Writing Ability

Most teachers who have taught at a particular grade level in the same school for several years have reached a judgment about the writing ability of their students. By experience they have learned what to expect from the students and what kinds of writing assignments will be most successful. For teachers new to a situation or for teachers about to try some new kinds of writing assignments, a more thorough assessment of student writing ability may be needed. This assessment might be one outcome of the first few informal writing assignments, or it might be a more deliberate activity. Although assessment, instruction, and evaluation are separate purposes for writing assignments, all three purposes may very well occur in the same assignment. Some preliminary assessment, however, should definitely precede the preparation of directions and teaching strategies for complex assignments such as research papers. In this way, the teacher knows not only what to expect but also knows what has to be taught in conjunction with the writing assignment.

WRITING PROBLEMS OF CONCERN TO CONTENT TEACHERS

Implicit in the variety of tasks suggested here is the realization that there are more things to look for in writing than spelling or punctuation errors, although such errors are very obvious and annoying. Every teacher is concerned about spelling and punctuation, but these errors do not usually go away simply because they are outlawed. The reason is that they may not always be caused by inattention or laziness. Sometimes errors indicate inexperience with reading or writing or both. Sometimes they are carry-overs from the dialect a student is used to hearing. Sometimes they indicate actual learning disabilities. Almost always they occur along with more serious writing difficulties that fall within the appropriate realm of concern for the content teacher. The more serious difficulties include:

1. Outright misunderstandings of content or concepts.
2. Inability to catch the main point.
3. Inability to analyze the material.
4. Reluctance to divide material into sub-groupings or categories.
5. Difficulty in seeing relevance, relationships, comparisons.
6. Inability to apply the material, make inferences about it, derive conclusions from it.
7. Lack of experience with the writing process.
8. Faulty strategies for organizing long pieces of writing.
9. Unfamiliarity with the extent of elaboration expected in academic writing to support generalizations.
10. Problems with the specialized vocabulary or appropriate tone of a particular discipline.
11. Inability to judge what a particular audience expects or needs to know.
12. Inadequate practice with research skills such as notetaking and documentation.
13. Rigidity in considering new ideas.
14. Carelessness in following directions.

These difficulties are more serious writing problems because, unlike errors in spelling, punctuation, and dialect, they cannot be corrected by an editor (or secretary) in the final stages of editing. They are also more serious because they keep students from thinking productively rather than merely keeping them from communicating "politely." Therefore, it is most important that content area teachers encourage practice in writing without getting unduly discouraged or inflexible about the more superficial traits of writing, remembering always that those traits are important for what else they indicate rather than in and of themselves. The most obvious errors may not represent the most serious problems.

In other words, the content teacher should be concerned about aspects of writing that affect learning the subject at hand. Record keeping aids memory. Reformulations encourage insights. Reports communicate information. Each kind of writing task offers valuable practice and involves the students actively. Each kind of writing task also builds on slightly different sub-skills and slightly different motivations. The content teacher will want to understand these differences.

All of this is not to say that content teachers should disregard inappropriate grammar, spelling, or punctuation, especially as they grade pieces of writing. The expectation of excellence, after all, helps to encourage excellence. But wherever possible content teachers should encourage revision rather than teach "rules." The content teacher can thus elicit meaningful writing practice and help develop constructive attitudes toward the process of writing.

HOW WRITING CONNECTS WITH OTHER FACTORS

As mentioned previously, there is a direct connection between personal attitudes and writing ability. In a sense, a classroom writer is trying out the role of scholar, a role that may or may not feel comfortable. In this regard it is well for content teachers to be aware of the relationship between writing and learning styles; also between teaching styles and learning styles.[1] Some teachers are more directive than others, some more willing to set up conditions which allow students to make decisions about what and how they learn. Given all the variations and combinations possible in teaching and learning styles, it seems self-evident that a variety of writing tasks, some highly structured, some open-ended, would accomplish more for a broader range of students, whether the purpose be assessment, instruction, or evaluation, than would a single kind of task.

Personality differences, rather than differences in ability, may very well affect how well students do on different types of writing tasks. For some students a one-time, in-class writing sample is not going to show their best effort because of the anxiety raised in this situation. For others a long-term project is going to require more discipline than they are used to marshalling. Still others may not make a piece of writing clear because they are retarded in the social skills, too shy to talk much, or not attuned to the needs of their readers. Each of these personality traits, then, may also figure into an assessment of the students' writing ability.

In addition to the attitudes and personality traits which affect writing, motivation can have a powerful effect. Whenever possible there should be some other purpose to the writing task than merely testing or practice. Valid communication situations, after all, require that the writer have something of value to say, something more about a topic that their readers know, and someone in particular to say it to. Certainly this cardinal principle of communication is violated more times than not in classroom writing where the reader (rather than the writer) is the one who is an expert. The more natural the communication situation, however, the more valid the assessment. Many of the following assessment ideas could be introduced inconspicuously as part of the regular classwork and used for some purpose in addition to assessment, such as initiating a class discussion.

INTERPRETING STANDARDIZED TEST SCORES

Although standardized tests do not measure writing ability directly, there is a widely accepted correlation between test scores and general writing ability. Specifically, there is a high correlation between writing ability and scores on IQ tests, reading tests, and study skills tests. Most schools and colleges maintain records of student scores on such tests.

The Educational Testing Service, which publishes the Scholastic Aptitude Tests (SAT's) and the American College Tests (ACT's), furnishes colleges with computerized profiles of the sub-test results and predictions of success for various courses. Someone in the school counseling department can probably help with the interpretation of standardized test scores. If not, Buros's *Mental Measurement Yearbook*,[2] available in most libraries, offers a good description and interpretation of each commercial standardized test.

Standardized test scores, it should be noted, are themselves under attack as insensitive indicators of student ability.[3] Standardized tests do not allow for cultural differences and do not reflect how the student might perform in a more natural setting with no time constraints. Nevertheless, a range of test scores may have considerable predictive reliability for the range of writing ability within a given class.

INFORMAL OBSERVATION

A better measure for teachers of content courses might be a cumulative impression built on informal responses to several kinds of writing tasks done early in the course. Such responses have the advantage of being content-specific rather than purely literary. If the tasks are carefully designed, they will elicit responses which will help the teacher decide what can be presumed and what must be directly taught in subsequent lessons. By analyzing the responses, a content teacher will be able to identify students with serious problems early in the course, referring them to specialists for extra help where such services are available. When the tasks are combined with small group activities, the sensitive teacher may even be able to assess matters of attitude and learning style.

STRUCTURED EVALUATION

Rather than collect a random or general notion of class ability, some teachers may wish to maintain a record of skills each student demonstrates. One way of doing this is to make a list of the kinds of skills that will be necessary for coming writing assignments and then to make a chart showing how well each student performs these skills on early, in-class writing tasks, such as on a first-day questionnaire. If there will be a research paper assigned later in the course, the teacher might list the sub-skills necessary for such a complicated task on a class record sheet and determine, either informally or in a specially designed task, whether each student has mastered these sub-skills.

There are several ways to determine just which sub-skills may indeed be needed for a complex writing task. One way, of course, is to derive a list on the basis of past experience in writing or grading similar tasks. A better way is to analyze two student papers, a successful one and an unsuccessful one. After comparing the two, make a list of the strategies apparently employed by the successful student and not by the unsuccessful one. Or you could complete the assignment yourself, taking care to note all the strategies you employ in the process of completing it.

Figure 3.1 represents a special list that a teacher could use to identify specific sub-skills in order to assess comprehension, organizing ability, experience with conventions, research skills, and mechanical accuracy. After a first-day questionnaire, for example, the teacher could simply check the appropriate box for the comprehension and mechanical accuracy sub-skills. Later observations could also be recorded on this same sheet.

The record of individual achievement could easily be translated into a class record by constructing a chart similar to the one in Figure 3.2 which lists skills necessary for research-paper writing. Any student who had scored "fair" or "poor" on the Individual Record Sheet (Figure 3.1) receives a checkmark for that skill on the class chart. By making a tally of checkmarks, the teacher can determine which sub-skills need extra work.

Teachers planning to make use of peer groups may wish to make charts similar to Figures 3.1 and 3.2 as a way of assessing discussion skills. After observing students at work in small groups, the teacher could rate each student on such skills as clarifying the task, making valuable contributions, building on what others say, and summarizing what others say. Individual checklists might then be converted into a Class Chart similar to the one devised for Figure 3.2. Chapter 2 offers more specific suggestions about how to initiate group work gradually, making initial assessment of these skills more of a gradual process.

FIGURE 3.1

CHECKLIST OF WRITING SKILLS NEEDED IN A
POLITICAL SCIENCE COURSE *

E Excellent   VG Very Good   G Good   F Fair   P Poor

	E	VG	G	F	P
Comprehension: Expressing main ideas					
Selecting relevant support					
Understanding similarities and differences among examples					
Organizing ability: Working from an outline					
Writing fully developed paragraphs					
Using transitional devices					
Experience with conventions: Using special terms correctly					
Taking an objective tone					
Present tense for principles, past tense for historical cases					
Research skills: Selecting relevant information					
Paraphrasing					
Documenting quotations					
Mechanical accuracy: Spelling names and terms correctly					
Standard verb forms					
Complete sentences					
*Easily adapted to other subjects.					

FIGURE 3.2

CLASS CHART OF WRITING SKILLS NECESSARY
IN WRITING RESEARCH PAPERS

Checkmarks indicate problem areas where work is needed.

Names of students	Using library	Finding relevant info	Notetaking	Paraphrasing	Quoting	Paragraphing	Outlining	Transitions	Spelling	Grammar
Abrams, John										
Blackburn, Donald										
Cirino, Lettie										
etc.										

SHORT, FOCUSED, IN-CLASS WRITING

The least conspicuous and least stressful way of assessing student writing ability is to collect frequent samples of informal or expressive writing done as a natural component of other class activities. By asking students at the end of a class to write what they remember from it, you can determine who caught the main points and what the misunderstandings were. By asking students to write down potential subheadings for a list of information given in class, you can determine who has the ability to categorize. Or by supplying students with several discrete, but related facts and asking them to write conclusions which could be drawn from them, you can elicit inferences and determine the ability to abstract. Indeed, you can gear the challenge of short in-class expressive writing to whatever skills you are interested in assessing. Other suggestions for informal writing tasks are offered in Chapters 2 and 4.

FIRST DAY QUESTIONNAIRE

Open-ended questions about the students' preconceptions of a course will elicit useful information as well as demonstrate writing ability. Figure 3.3 is a sample questionnaire for a United States Government class, but the types of questions asked are easily adapted to other subjects. This questionnaire was designed to assess vocabulary, ability to categorize (question 1), skill at formulating comparisons and support of generalizations (question 2), perception of relevance (question 3), and adoption of appropriate voice (question 4). Because whole sentences are called for, the teacher will also be able to judge mechanical accuracy. If questions are answered too briefly, the teacher may recognize some attitude problems or even some reading difficulties, since the short answer may indicate a question was misunderstood. As an additional bonus from the questionnaire, the teacher may have valid nominations for class speakers.

    Before interpreting the responses, the teacher may want students to share them in small groups. Through discussion it could be determined whether bizarre groupings in question 1 result from misunderstandings of the terms or inappropriate categories (for a governmental context). For example, someone might group *conservative*, *Communist*, and *Castro* together because they all begin with C. Such a student needs more practice with categorizing. Similarly, students who pick obvious points of similarity in question 3 (e.g., both are governments) or bizarre similarities (e.g., both use public buildings) may need further small-group work with drawing inferences. Responses to the last three questions will provide evidence of language discrimination and experience. Are words given in context spelled correctly? If not, the student will need practice in editing. Do the sentences sound natural? If not, the student is probably extremely apprehensive about writing. Does the last answer sound like a speech? If not, the student will need work on judging appropriate tone and level of diction for a given purpose. What about left out words or letter reversals? They are definitely proof-reading problems and could be indicative of learning disabilities.[4]

FIGURE 3.3

SAMPLE FIRST-DAY QUESTIONNAIRE FOR POLITICAL SCIENCE*

NAME _____ COURSE _____ HOUR _____

1. In the space below arrange these words into several lists; then briefly explain why you grouped the words in each list together: Republican, Democrat, liberal, Communist, moderate, Socialist, conservative, right-wing, left-wing, Fidel Castro, Richard Nixon, Franklin D. Roosevelt

2. What is the biggest difference between our school government and our city government? Explain your answer in several sentences.

3. Name a relative, acquaintance, or local personality who could be interviewed on some topic related to government:

   _____

   Briefly explain the person's qualifications and the kind of information he or she could provide:

4. Pretend you are running for governor. Make the beginning of a short speech telling what you will do about the environment if you are elected.

*Easily adapted to other subjects.

Other structured, individualized approaches to writing assessment might be more specifically correlated with the content to be studied. The teacher can invent a task with several different questions, each designed to elicit a type of writing appropriate to that discipline. A brief description of some of the individualized approaches follow.

CLOZE PROCEDURES

Cloze is a shortened version of the word *closure*. Cloze procedures are a way of determining a student's sense of closure or completeness about the language; in other words, how sensitive a student is to various contextual clues. Originally designed to assess the degree of difficulty a student might have with reading the textbook in a given course,[5] cloze procedures can also be used to assess the student's general familiarity with the regularities of sentence structure and vocabulary in a given subject. Cloze procedures measure a student's sense of language expectations by having the student guess at which words are missing in a passage copied from a book with every fifth word deleted.

To construct a cloze procedure, a passage of approximately 300 words should be typed with the first and last sentences intact and with uniform spaces left for each deleted word. Students should not be able to guess at the missing word on the basis of length. Sometimes, of course, the missing word will simply be an article; at other times the word will be a proper noun the student will have no way of knowing. Therefore, students are expected to get only about 50 percent of the answers correct (with the exact word from the passage). Students who get fewer than 40 percent of the words correct will have great difficulty in reading the textbook from which the passage was drawn and may have difficulty writing at the appropriate level of formality on class assignments.

The advantage of the cloze procedure is that it can be graded in class by class members with follow-up discussion of the clues inherent in the passage. Also, the task is directly correlated with the content of the course. The cloze procedure is particularly useful in teaching fiction or poetry, since it predicts ability to read at the level of the assigned reading and also encourages attention to word choices and connotation.

One disadvantage of the procedure is that it only predicts success or difficulty in a general way and does not in itself suggest any specific remediation exercises. Another disadvantage is that students invariably feel angry when they find they cannot "get credit" for synonyms. The reason for this rule is that the percentages are meant to allow for "near misses," it being too difficult to judge appropriate and inappropriate synonyms. Part of the reason for the anger is confusion

FIGURE 3.4
_____

SAMPLE CLOZE PROCEDURE

Figure 2-2 shows the relationship between the three principal genetic classes of rocks: igneous, sedimentary, and metamorphic rocks. This relationship is known _____ the rock cycle. Igneous _____ form by the cooling _____ hardening of melted materials. (_____ Figure 2-3.) The word "igneous" _____ from the Latin word _____ fire. Igneous rocks and _____ kinds of rocks exposed _____ the surface of the _____ are subject to weathering. _____ involves both the chemical _____ physical breakdown of _____ exposed to the atmosphere _____ hydrosphere at the earth's _____ .

The weathered rock that _____ on the earth's surface _____ continually moved by water, _____ , and ice. This process _____ moving materials is known _____ erosion. Erosion eventually carries _____ of the broken-down _____ material to the oceans _____ it is spread in _____ of sediments as shown _____ Figure 2-4.

The sands and _____ sediments that make up _____ beaches extend out along _____ bottom of the sea. _____ time they are covered _____ other sediments and may _____ pressed together to form _____ _____ . Such rocks are called _____ rocks. Sedimentary rocks can _____ from any type of _____ that happens to be _____ at the earth's surface. (_____ Figure 2-2.)

Metamorphic rocks are _____ from rocks that are _____ or pressed together under _____ pressure for long periods _____ time. They form deep _____ the surface of the _____ . Bricks are made by _____ and heating blocks of _____ clay. In somewhat the _____ way metamorphic rocks form _____ sedimentary rocks. They may _____ form from igneous rocks. _____ type of metamorphic rock _____ depends on the amount _____ heat and pressure and the composition of the rock being changed. *Metamorphic* comes from Greek words for change and form.

FIGURE 3.4 (continued)

SAMPLE CLOZE PROCEDURE

MISSING WORDS

as, rocks, and, See, comes, for, other, at, earth, Weathering, and, rock, and, surface, collects, is, wind, of, as, much, rock, where, layers, in, other, our, the, In, by, become, rock, sedimentary, form, rock, at, See, formed, heated, high, of, beneath, earth, pressing, soft, same, from, also, The, formed, of

Source: Reprinted with permission from Earth Science Curriculum Project, *Investigating the Earth* (Boston: Houghton Mifflin Company, 1967), 38.

over differences between this type of diagnostic tool and a "fill-in-the-blanks" test, where right and wrong answers measure something else. Sometimes a warning ahead of time about the synonym problem will prevent misdirected anger. The cloze activity can be easily turned into a lesson in vocabulary or grammar by deleting just those words which are likely to cause difficulty for the students.

REFORMULATION EXERCISES

With reformulation exercises the student is asked to convert something graphic—a chart or illustration—into words. Again the graphic representation could be taken directly from the textbook. An interesting variation on this is to have half the class convert the graphic representation into words and the other half convert a paragraph description into something visual. Follow-up discussion should focus on the characteristics of clear writing and the gaps in information that some representations may have left with puzzled readers.

However, there are problems with interpreting the reformulation. Break-downs in communication could derive from misreadings of the original or misunderstandings of the material rather than writing problems per se. Although the activity generally reveals problems with forming generalizations or considering the reader's needs (egocentricity), it is difficult to isolate these variables from the total experience. Reformulation activities will identify your more experienced and less experienced writers and also furnish valuable practice for later writing tasks.

In Figure 3.5 the science student is asked to convert some data about elasticity of gases into a written description. To make that reformulation clear, the student will have to visualize the original demonstration and then describe it. In this case the task is complicated by a graph that is confusing because it does not visually reinforce the concept of compression. The line rises with each addition of weight whereas the cylinders they refer to and resemble visually would have gotten smaller with each addition of weight. Further, the terminology of the graph is specialized (bricks for weights). To do well on this task, students have to perceive and articulate certain basic relationships: that all three gases compressed to the same extent, and that they compressed more in response to the first weight than they did proportionately with the addition of subsequent weights. As the directions make clear, to get full credit students would have to state a generalization about the graph and some statistical support.

The teacher may discover that problems with reading prevent a student from doing reformulations at all. Students must be able to read charts and graphs before they can perceive the intended relationships. The specialized technical terms might also pose problems. Only minimally would problems of sentence structure, spelling, or punctuation interfere with success or failure on this reformulation task.

Incidentally, the reformulation task is a good one for illustrating the value of writing for learning. It is only by describing a graph or chart that one can study it well enough to perceive the relationships in it.

FIGURE 3.5

INFORMATION SUITABLE FOR CONVERSION TO ANOTHER FORM

DIRECTIONS:
The following chart and graph are representations of information recorded when three gases were compressed in cylinders. Weights, called bricks, were placed on the tops of the cylinders to make the gas compress. Your job is to study these illustrations and then write a one-paragraph description of what the demonstration tells us about the elasticity of gases. Remember that you will have to interpret the information, not just state the numbers.

Mass (bricks)	Air		Propane		Carbon Dioxide	
	Volume (cm^3)	Decrease in volume (cm^3)	Volume (cm^3)	Decrease in volume (cm^3)	Volume (cm^3)	Decrease in volume (cm^3)
0	35.0	0.0	35.0	0.0	35.0	0.0
1	23.2	11.8	23.2	11.8	23.1	11.9
2	17.3	17.7	17.4	17.6	17.3	17.7
3	13.7	21.3	13.6	21.4	13.8	21.2
4	11.2	23.8	11.2	23.8	11.2	23.8
5	9.7	25.3	9.5	25.5	9.7	25.3
6	8.3	26.7	8.2	26.8	8.3	26.8

Source: From Haber-Schaim, Uri, et al, *Introductory Physical Science*, 2nd ed. (Englewood Cliffs, NJ: Prentice-Hall, Inc., 1972), 43. Reprinted with permission.

FIGURE 3.5 (continued)

INFORMATION SUITABLE FOR CONVERSION TO ANOTHER FORM

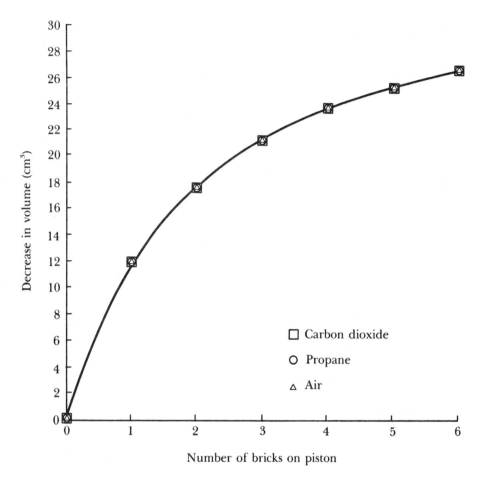

SUMMARY PARAGRAPHS

Another context-specific assessment task involves retelling the main points of a complicated piece of writing. Students can be asked to summarize a passage read to them. Reading the passage aloud will prevent the possibility of students copying the piece or large parts of it. However, if the directions clearly state the need either to rephrase groups of words or copy them deliberately using quotation marks, then there is value in having the students work from a written text. The value of this type of exercise is that it indirectly measures comprehension as well as the ability to condense major ideas. Figure 3.6 represents a passage suitable for summarizing.

FIGURE 3.6

PASSAGE APPROPRIATE FOR SUMMARY ASSESSMENT

Human beings are social animals, which means that they live in various kinds of groups, big and small. Some human groups are so small that they include only a few families; others may extend to thousands of people. Within each group, the kind and number of relationships vary. Living in groups is itself neither unusual nor unexpected. Many kinds of mammals live in herds or prides or troops. And our closest nonhuman relatives among the mammals, the higher primates, are all committed to life with others of their kind. Such animals as baboons and gorillas, capuchin monkeys and chimpanzees all spend their lives within earshot and seeing distance of fairly specific groups.

In fact, there are many indications that a monkey or a gorilla who is raised apart from a group does not grow up to behave in a way typical of his kind. He becomes a pathological specimen, frequently unable to mate as an adult or to take proper care of children if mating has been achieved. The traits that make for successful group living have been selected for over time, which seems to indicate that living in groups has great advantages for primates otherwise unequipped with really formidable physical defenses.

Looking in on a group of monkeys or chimpanzees can be a truly startling experience for a thoughtful observer. In zoos, these animals are very popular, and many people find their behavior amusing. But how they are organized, how they behave, how they act and react are all amusing, not because they are so foreign, but because their behavior uncannily resembles that of the human beings who watch them. They are like us, but they are somehow different, and in the difference rests their comical appeal.

What is the basic difference between human groups and monkey and ape groups? To anthropologists the gulf between the most complex monkey groups and the simplest human society is the fact that the behavior of the human group depends on culture while that of the monkey group does not. When anthropologists use the term "culture," they are generally referring to the traditional social heritage of mankind or to the traditional social heritage of one segment of it, a single culture or society. Culture consists of all the ideas, sentiments, patterns of behavior, ways of doing things, thoughts, actions, and objects that an individual has access to as a result of being born a human being in a human group.

Source: Reprinted with permission from Carol Mason, Martin Harry Greenberg, and Patricia Warrick, Editors, *Anthropology through Science Fiction* (New York: St. Martin's Press, 1974), 121–122.

This passage, from an anthropology textbook, is appropriate because it can be understood out of context and because it is interesting material. The main point is clear, but presented inductively so that readers can be led to the wrong conclusions by allowing their preconceptions to intrude upon what is literally stated, a tendency encouraged by the rather lengthy subordinate sentence structures characterizing this passage. Also, the terminology is sufficiently context-specific to present potential problems.

Figures 3.7 and 3.8 represent appropriate and inappropriate summary responses to this passage. Figure 3.7 is successful because the main ideas are preserved while unimportant details are left out.

FIGURE 3.7

AN APPROPRIATE SUMMARY*

Humans, like many other animals, are social. That is, they live in groups ranging in size from a few to thousands. Baboons, gorillas, monkeys, and chimps are not normal if they are raised outside the group. Human groups are different, however, in that they depend on culture — "all the ideas, sentiments, patterns of behavior, ways of doing things, thoughts, actions, and objects that an individual has access to as a result of being part of that human group."

Its Good Points:
1. Main ideas reflected accurately
2. Unimportant or illustrative details left out
3. Emphasis consistent with the original
4. Specialized terms noted (social, culture, etc.)
5. Quotation marks used to mark copied portions

*Based on Figure 3.6

The emphasis is consistent with the original passage. Furthermore, the specialized terms are noted and the definition of the most important term, *culture*, is quoted.

Figure 3.8 is inappropriate because the main idea was misunderstood. This writer emphasized the similarities of primates to humans rather than their differences. In doing so, the writer also exaggerated unimportant details so as to change the emphasis of the original passage. Specialized terms, such as *social*, were construed in their general sense rather than in their specialized sense. Finally, sections of the text were copied without benefit of quotation marks. If this student's performance was recorded on a record sheet, such as the one pictured in Figure 3.1, it would be evident that several sub-skills needed further work before a research paper could be assigned.

Of course in real life, either of these summaries might also have contained misspellings and other inaccuracies of varying seriousness. In all likelihood the inappropriate summary would contain more

FIGURE 3.8
_____

AN INAPPROPRIATE SUMMARY*

Human beings like to socialize. In this way they are very similar to monkeys. They are unable sometimes to mate or take care of children. They take time to achieve successful group living and develop really formidable physical defenses. Looking at a group of monkeys or chimpanzees can indeed be a truly startling experience.

Its Bad Points:
1. Main ideas misunderstood (similarity to primates emphasized rather than differences)
2. Unimportant details overemphasized
3. Emphasis changed to focus on primates
4. Misapplied specialized terms (social became socialize with its conversational meaning)
5. Sections copied rather than paraphrased

*Based on Figure 3.6

mistakes than the appropriate summary. The point is that those mistakes would be in addition to the features that make for good or bad content summaries.

NOTES ON A LECTURE

Without specifying a format, the teacher could announce that notes would be collected at the end of a particular lecture day, perhaps when a guest lecturer is present (so that the teacher, too, could take notes). This experience might set the stage for a lesson in notetaking in addition to serving as an assessment in and of itself. Some traits to look for might include clear spacing; the elimination of "filler" words; meaningful groupings (not necessarily outline form); inclusion of some detail, but not too much: accurate understandings. Figure 3.9 represents good notetaking ability.

In Figure 3.9 the notes are dated and labeled for later reference. The information and emphasis are correct, with main points covered

FIGURE 3.9

GOOD LECTURE NOTES

10/2 *Psyche* : Terms Describing Experiments

Large experiment
(1930): tracing
star in mirror .

variable - single factor
 which can be isolated

amount of rest
between tries

independent variable -
 factor which is
 manipulated

task and no. of
tries

dependent variables -
 factors held constant

3 treatment groups
 no rest
 24 - hour rest
 20 - day rest

experimental group - subjects
 who receive treatment
 (manipulated variable)

all had same task
and no. of tries

control group - subjects
 similar except for
 special treatment

Good Points:
1. Date and title provided
2. Information and emphasis correct
3. Main points covered, unimportant details left out
4. Enough specific details for easy reference later
5. Clear spacing to reinforce relationships

and details left out. However, enough details are included for easy reference later. The clear spacing reinforces the relationships inherent in the material.

Figure 3.10, by contrast, represents inadequate notetaking ability. No date or title is provided. A reader could not tell that the lecture was the same one that inspired the notes of Figure 3.9. In Figure 3.10 the information is not representative of the lecture. Some important main points about terminology are left out. Instead, the notes exaggerate the importance of what had been, apparently, an "aside" on the part of the lecturer; how to perform the experiment at home. Yet there aren't any specific details for later reference. Furthermore, the paragraph form is confusing visually.

Although notes are normally taken for the benefit of the person who is taking them, they should be clear enough to make some sense to a person with similar background who may have been absent from class. Too often students assume they will remember more than they

---

FIGURE 3.10

INADEQUATE LECTURE NOTES

Factors cause a certain result, such as the independent variable being manipulated. People had to trace a star design using a mirror. They were given different lengths of time between tries. Use cardboard and a shaving mirror to try this at home. No rest, 24 hour, and 20 days. Experiment wouldn't have worked if task familiar. e.g. shaving in mirror or copying a series of letters. Best job by subjects with lots of practice.

Bad Points:
1. No date or title provided
2. Information misunderstood, emphasis not representative of the lecture
3. Some main points left out, unimportant things exaggerated
4. No details for later reference
5. Paragraph form confusing visually

do; they fail to take down enough information for the notes to make sense to them after a lapse of time. At the other extreme are students who fail to sift main points and feel frustrated because they can't keep up in their efforts to take down every word. Notetaking is further discussed in later chapters.

SPECIALIZED VOCABULARY

There are three things about vocabulary study that must be considered in assessing student ability. First, words appear in context and must be used with their special assumed features, not always mentioned in the dictionary definition of the term. For example, the word *dubious* is used with *of* or *about*. The following sentence would be wrong, therefore, even though *dubious* does mean *doubtful,* as the writer of the sentence knew: "I am dubious at those scores." In this regard, teachers need to be sensitive to the problems of new words, pronouncing them as well as writing them in sentences. Second, the hardest words are those which have a generalized meaning in other settings and thus cause confusion for the student just being introduced to a new discipline. Such words include *value* in math and *point of view* in literature. And, third, new words are learned most willingly when there is a recognizable purpose for the learning. For example, a set of directions with specialized terms in it, accompanied by a set of brief definitions, will teach the words better than any isolated list of new terms when these specialized terms have to be understood so that the directions can be followed. Any realistic vocabulary test will allow for these three word problems.

Some ways to assess vocabulary skill are to have students construct sentences using a word given in context elsewhere, or to set up a situation where the student must use the same word in two ways. Examples of the latter technique appear in Figure 3.11.

One value of vocabulary assessment is that the very process of focusing on words makes students sensitive to them in context, even when they are not directly studied thereafter.

RESEARCH SKILLS

In a biology class, the teacher might organize several small-group activities to determine which students had already mastered the research skills not covered by the first-day questionnaire. Figure 3.12 illustrates sample tasks which might form the basis of the assessment of abilities for several sub-skills needed for research in a science class.

FIGURE 3.11

VOCABULARY ASSESSMENT

DIRECTIONS:
Using your algebra book as a reference, interpret each of the following sentences in two ways. The first one is done for you.

Sentence	What the Average Person on the Street Thinks Sentence Means:	What Students in Algebra II Know the Sentence Means:
1. We will write some equality statements.	We are interested in civil rights.	The numbers on each side of an equal sign have to total the same amount.
2. I see a prime number.		
3. What are the factors of that product?		
4. Name a useful property of sums.		
5. The problem consisted of like terms.		

Source: Based on Chapter 1 in Irving Drooyan and William Wooton, *Elementary Algebra with Geometry* (New York: John Wiley & Sons, Inc., 1976).

The first task reveals who can discriminate between relevant and extraneous information and who can take good notes. The second exercise has the additional virtues of eliciting a perception of similarities or differences and measuring experience with documentation. Both activities also provide information about mechanical accuracy.

It should be pointed out that discussions growing out of tasks such as those described in Figure 3.9 will be learning experiences as well as assessment procedures. Students will come to realize where their misunderstandings occurred. They will be expanding their language experience through the practice they gain in explaining orally and listening with a purpose. Ideally, peers will teach peers how to use quotations. A handout about quotations or a handbook should be available for reference.

DOCUMENTATION CONVENTIONS

High school students and college students should be able to convert direct quotations into indirect ones and vice versa. They may need a reminder, however, as to how quotations are punctuated or documented. The best way to test for this is to offer models for imitation. Rarely do such conventions have to be memorized because, theoretically at least, students always have access to reference books.

For documentation tasks the problems to be concerned with are the ability to distinguish between restatements and original statements, between oral statements and written statements (both called quotations when used by a writer), and between one documentation format and another. Figure 3.13 represents a documentation exercise where a model is provided, but the student still has a difficult job. Not only must the student understand the content, he or she also must use this information to support an original main idea. Additionally, there is a problem of focus: few students will attend to all features of the documentation format even though a model is provided.

FIGURE 3.12

SAMPLE TASKS ASSESSING WRITING SKILLS NECESSARY FOR WRITING RESEARCH PAPERS*

DIRECTIONS:
Your group should prepare a review of one chapter of our textbook for the rest of the class. Each individual should take notes on one section of the chapter and then come together to construct a one-page summary combining your information. Each member will submit individual contributions as well as the group overview.

OR

DIRECTIONS:
Here is a newspaper story which contradicts some of the facts given in Chapter 3. Quote one sentence from the newspaper story and a short selection from Chapter 3 which seems to present an opposite view. Briefly explain the differences your quotations suggest. Be sure to mention the author and source of each quotation.

*Both of these tasks can become the basis of discussion within and between groups, explaining and justifying choices.

FIGURE 3.13

SAMPLE EVALUATION FORM FOR DOCUMENTATION

DIRECTIONS:
Below is a title page, a portion of a book, and a paragraph which summarizes the information and quotes parts of the content in answer to a question. The quotation is documented. Your job is to look closely at this information. Then study the similar information given below. Your job will be to write a summary paragraph similar to the one given. You should also choose a sentence to quote and document it. Pay special attention to order, spacing, and punctuation.

Applied Fluid Mechanics Robert L. Mott Charles E. Merrill Publishing Co. Columbus, Ohio 1972	p. 63 Buoyancy is the tendency for a fluid to exert a supporting force on a body placed in the fluid. This force is called a buoyant force . . .

Question: What is buoyancy?

Buoyancy is another word for floating ability. A body floats in a liquid because of a force equal to the weight of the liquid it displaces. As one textbook states, "Buoyancy is the tendency for a fluid to exert a supporting force on a body placed in the fluid" (Mott, 63).

Birds of North America Chandler S. Robbins Bertel Bruun Herbert S. Zim Golden Press New York 1966	p. 6 Birding amply satisfies our curiosity about all animal life. The joys of discovery and the aesthetic appeal of avian species provide rewarding experiences for the observer . . .

Question: Why do people study birds?

If the students given a documentation task are writing reports based on interviews and conversations, the teacher might include some practice in converting questions into statements and vice versa. Many students, even at the college level, have trouble with this reformulation, especially as some dialects do not make the full transformation. For example, some dialects do not completely transform the direction question, "Can you perform?" into the indirect question, "She asked if I could perform." Instead, speakers of this dialect might say (with the same inflection of voice as the speaker above), "She asked could I perform." Students regularly speaking such dialects would have to accumulate experience with the structure of the standard transformation through reading. Discriminations such as these bring out the differences between talk and writing and between informal and formal writing. It is better to stress those descriptions instead of using terms like "right" and "wrong," since a person's use of the language is so closely tied to his or her sense of self.

OBJECTIVITY AND FORMAL TONE

The assessment of writing should include some measure of a student's ability to revise. One good method of doing this is to have the student revise a casual or conversational piece of writing into something more suitable for the academic style of writing. Figure 3.14 offers a sample of such a task and could become the basis for further discussion or study of other examples.

Figure 3.15 is a successful revision. It is based on a scholarly passage from a history textbook. Lofty phrases were simply translated into clichés and informal banalities in a process which, in effect, reverses what the student will now be asked to do. The student's revision, of course, should preserve the main ideas without adding new ones. The revised version should simply contain straightforward explanation without the informal phraseology of the exercise passage. Of course, the revision should be accurate mechanically as well.

If students have trouble doing this exercise, they probably lack experience reading in the content area and should be required to do more reading before they are instructed directly in the traits of academic discourse.

As a final capstone on this exercise, the class might look at the original text and compare it with what they have each written. Ironically, they could discover a directness and naturalness in their own version which is not characteristic of the so-called model from which it was drawn. The realization that writers have rhetorical options might be the added bonus to this type of assessment. Another bonus is the hidden message that revision is a means of making choices rather than a punishment "for not writing well the first time." The disadvan-

FIGURE 3.14
_____

PASSAGE SUITABLE FOR ASSESSMENT OF REVISION STRATEGIES

DIRECTIONS:
Re-write the following passage so that it conveys the same information, but reads more like a textbook.

The Industrial Revolution hasn't got a good name. Not a revolution and not really industrial. We used to think the dates were 1760–1830, more or less. You can now see them starting earlier and continued beyond. Technical developments in agriculture and industry were part of the picture. The open-field system of agriculture evaporated. The domestic system for organizing industries also went the way of all flesh, and factories came into being. The results was economic changes causing many of today's problems economically, socially, and politically speaking.

Changes to look for:
1. The main idea should stay the same.
2. The informal phrases should be eliminated (e.g., hasn't got a good name, way of all flesh, evaporated, more or less, the results is, etc.).
3. Changes in person should be changed to third person only.
4. Awkward modification should be simplified, especially in the last sentence.

Source: Based on W.E. Lunt, *History of England*, 4th Edition (New York: Harper and Brothers, 1957), 564–565.

_____

tage of this activity is that there are no absolute right or wrong responses, and this realization might be frustrating both for teachers and for students.

THE PAYOFFS OF ASSESSMENT

Once content teachers are aware of the complexity of writing tasks and the strengths and weaknesses of their students, they may see the need for more writing in their courses. What is learned from the assessment may show up in shorter, more focused assignments. Or there may be such a wide range of writing ability within a single class that individualized writing assignments are called for. Another result of assessment might be the incorporation of more discussion and record keeping in class as warm-ups for the more complicated, formal assignments. In cases where severe writing problems are evident, content teachers may wish to work with support services at the school, such as the writing tutors in a writing lab. Seeing a tutor may even become a requirement in the content course rather than a mere recommendation.

FIGURE 3.15

ACCEPTABLE REVISION

Based on Figure 3.14

The Industrial Revolution is misnamed because it was not merely industrial, nor was it really a revolution. Furthermore, the period extended longer than from 1760–1830 as previously understood. During that time technical developments in agriculture and industry resulted in vast economic changes. For example, the open-field system of agriculture disappeared. Also, factories replaced domestic systems of production. Many of today's economic, social, and political problems can be traced to these economic changes.

Additionally, content teachers may want to find out from the English department what handbooks or dictionaries are used at the school and supply the content classrooms with some of these for reference when problems arise.

No matter what the assessment findings or how many resources may be available for students to use, the best indoctrination into the writing expected in a content course is exposure to models of good student writing. Always keep copies of acceptable papers and let students use them as a part of their regular coursework. More will be learned about appropriate style that way than by any amount of direct instruction.

Certainly a content teacher who assesses will become aware of the need for "walking students through" complex assignments, concentrating on clear directions, perhaps requiring rough drafts along the way. Another outcome might be the decision to "publish" model papers or sample papers, perhaps including discussion of these in the regular pattern of coursework. The chapters which follow offer additional practical suggestions for incorporating some of these plans into the content coverage of a particular course. There are also suggestions for assigning writing tasks that build on what the students have demonstrated they can do. As students become more involved, morale will improve for both teachers and students.

NOTES

1. For more extended discussions of learning styles see Adaia Shumsky, "Individual Differences in Learning Styles," in *Learning Performance and Individual Differences*, ed. by Len Sperry (Glenview, Illinois: Scott, Foresman and Company, 1972), pp. 122–125; also, Kenneth Hoover, *The Professional Teacher's Handbook: A Guide for Improving Instruction in Today's Middle and Secondary Schools* (Boston: Allyn and Bacon, 1976), 66–67.

2. O.K. Buros, *The Seventh Annual Mental Measurement Yearbook* (Highland Park, NJ: The Gryphon Press, 1972).

3. See, for example, H.C. Rudman, "Standardized Test Flap," *Phi Delta Kappan* 49 (March 1978): 470–471.

4. For a complete discussion of what learning disabilities are see Janet W. Lerner, *Children with Learning Disabilities* (Boston: Houghton Mifflin Company, 1971).

5. For an explanation of how cloze procedures work see W.S. Taylor, "Cloze Procedures: A New Tool for Measuring Reading," *Journalism Quarterly* 30 (Fall 1953): 415–433.

4

Record-Keeping
Tasks

It is well known that the brain can only hold a limited number of discrete items in short-term memory simultaneously. That number is variously held to be five, plus or minus two.[1] Lectures go by at a much greater rate than can be remembered, and textbooks, too, present more facts than can be absorbed as quickly as they can be read. Writing in the form of notetaking can serve as an external memory. The very act of writing enhances attention and so promotes comprehension. Furthermore, writing triggers the kinds of associations and connections that integrate new learning with previous experience.

NOTETAKING ON LECTURES AND BOOKS

Good notes are useful both for information retrieval and as a means of comprehending the material as it is transmitted. Yet notes represent highly personal ways of synthesizing material. One person's way of recording information may not necessarily help another person recall the lecture or reading that the notes were based on. This is so because people chunk information differently and telescope long sentences differently. Thus the process of notetaking reinforces idiosyncratic ways of categorizing and summarizing material, and students need to feel comfortable with their own way of doing these two elementary things before they can undertake more complex tasks, such as research papers.

Recent research shows that good students not only record information, but also respond to the information and jot down questions about it as they write.[2] Such students are more likely to participate in discussions and ask questions in class than others.

Ineffective students, on the other hand, are often convinced that they will remember the material without recording it. They may even be convinced that they cannot listen or read as well when they are simultaneously writing. Teachers, when aware of these problems, sometimes slow down their lectures to a writing pace in an attempt to help students take notes in outline form. Such practices can make for boring lessons and the elimination of interesting anecdotes and illustrations. Students are prevented from having to telescope information and write while listening. Similarly, certain short cuts on book notetaking may prove to be counter-productive. Underlining or highlighting passages (when permitted) can become automatic and does not assure assimilation of the material.

One problem in encouraging notetaking is motivation. Being graded on notes—or on cumulative notebooks—may or may not be sufficient motivation to do well, especially for less able students. A better tactic is to build natural rewards into the notetaking process.

Since notes are written primarily to oneself, the most natural motivation might arise from making some discovery or coming to some new insight while writing notes and because of writing notes. Ideally these insights represent the key concepts of the course, arrived at inductively. For example, from a physics experiment a student may come to the realization that electrical current in a circuit varies with the resistance if the voltage is constant. Discovering this kind of concept experientially and recording the discovery in writing seems to have a different, deeper effect on a learner than being given the concepts verbally in their abstract forms. Chapter 2 contains more ideas about how to encourage short, focused responses to new information and as a means of consciously integrating old information with new. Sometimes it is worth the time to pause midway through a lecture to allow students a few minutes for speculative writing in response to directions such as, "Take a few minutes to write quickly some comments on, questions about, or applications of what we have been considering today. There are no right or wrong answers, but some of you might later like to read what you have written out loud to the class."

In the above case students are expanding their sense of audience for notes and responses to include their peers and their teachers. Other ways of expanding their sense of audience and, at the same time, indirectly, of demonstrating the limitations of relying on someone else's notes without the fuller experience that the notes were based on, would be to set up situations where students take notes for each other. Students can take turns preparing notes for classmates, who, for one reason or another, are absent on a certain day. These "public notes" can be kept in the classroom and used by students instead of each one individually asking the teacher what they missed. In fact, class notes can be kept for activities and discussions as well as lectures. Another idea is to have different groups be responsible for different parts of a textbook, taking notes in duplicate or on ditto for swapping with their classmates. This last process, incidentally, would promote critical appraisal of notetaking as each group needs to make sure it understood the other groups' notes. Comparisons of notes or note swaps could lead to a small group project growing out of the information contained in the notes.

An example of a project growing out of notetaking might be a "Word Problem Bee" in Algebra class. The students are directed to write the general principles involved in a set of word problems. Then they meet in class in small groups to compare their understanding of the general principles, so they can then make up new word problems based on these same principles. The word problems will be given to individuals on an opposing team made up of another small group, the members of which have also gone through the same process and are ready with their own set of word problems. The teacher awards points for problems which truly illustrate the principles involved and for quick solutions to the problems written by opposing teams.

Although occasional games or projects like this one may promote interest in taking good notes, the most natural use for notes involves private information retrieval. Problems or questions may come up in class that require looking something up in notes. Sometimes a situation can be deliberately contrived to require this. For example, a discussion question, such as the one listed below, might follow a unit on Ibo culture in Anthropology class:

> How many times have we mentioned something which would also be true of Navaho culture?

A question involving this much thought and discrimination would require more than a quick counting of items for an answer and so would be ideal for a short-focused in-class writing prior to any oral discussion of the answer.

Notes could also be used for all or part of a test situation built on higher-order tasks than mere recall. (See Figure 4.10 for examples of analysis and evaluation questions which could be asked to take advantage of good notes to be referred to during the test situation itself.)

SQ3R

The kinds of notes taken on books will vary with the subject matter and the follow-up activities or test situations. For most textbooks a variation on the SQ3R approach would be appropriate.[3] The formula

SQ3R stands for *s*urvey, *q*uestion, *r*ead, *r*eview, and *r*ecite. Students first survey the material (look through it quickly), then question it (turn the headings or topic sentences into verbal thought questions which will be answered by reading on). These two processes give the student some focus for reading. As they read, students review the main ideas or most important facts. Finally, they recite (preferably in writing) what they remember (without looking back). The kinds of information they record or recite will, of course, vary. Figure 4.1 represents an SQ3R approach to Chapter 3 of this book. It records the hypothetical thoughts of a reader. The recitation list, however, should actually be written out. That list clearly is different from regular notes; it represents cryptic references to things remembered. Knowing that the reading will lead to such a list allows the information to register at a deeper level than would be the case otherwise. Most students, however, might still have to go back and take notes.

THE "HIDDEN CURRICULUM"

The kinds of information recorded in notes will depend primarily on clues students have picked up directly or indirectly from their teachers. Since most textbooks contain more information than any reader could possibly retain, teachers should give some thought to giving students a focus, some guidelines for selecting the essential information. Teachers often do this indirectly, of course, by revealing their values in lectures and class discussion. Good students are often very successful at tuning into this "hidden curriculum," meaning the way the teacher's mind sees relationships or the way a given discipline dictates that relationships be perceived and remembered.

In psychology, for instance, the notes and record-keeping tasks are often terms with definitions or names of famous psychologists and what they are known for. The act of writing these tends to imprint them in memory. The act of responding to them (i.e., reciting) serves to involve students in seeing or questioning relationships among discrete forms of information. In history the notes will often be trends or movements characterizing an era. Again, the act of writing them will help students perceive the way they fit together into the overall relationships of the "hidden curriculum."

OUTLINING

Even though there may be specific notetaking tasks associated with the different disciplines, there are also generalized systems which can be adapted to almost any discipline or course. The most common of

FIGURE 4.1

SQ3R APPLIED TO CHAPTER 3 OF THIS BOOK

MENTAL PROCESSES:

Survey
(flipping pages) Umm . . . looks like a lot of worksheets which could be used without many changes. . . . don't believe in standardized test scores myself. . . . These don't look like lists, more like assignments. Good thing there's a section on payoffs—the rest of this chapter looks like a lot of work!

Question
(formulated by turning headings and statements into questions) Why are these considered the most serious writing difficulties? How do test scores correlate with writing ability? What can be learned about writing from informal observation? Will record-keeping be too much of a chore? What is a Cloze procedure? How can notetaking be considered assessment? Are vocabulary and documentation matters for teachers like me?

Read
(skimming the content of the assessment instruments except for the titles, reading the rest carefully) Umm . . . gives credit to experienced teachers for already having some ideas about writing. I like the idea that mechanical errors co-occur with more serious errors. Umm . . . I never thought of academic writing as role playing . . . urges analysis of tasks to see what skills are needed . . . never realized before how many skills involved in term paper writing . . . good idea to have school-wide reference books available.

Review and Recite
(actually accomplished by writing down the things that are remembered—without looking back)

standardized tests, in-class informal writing, questionnaires (categorizing), charts of subskills, cloze procedures (anger), reformulation (charts/writing, etc.), summarizing (specialized vocabulary), notetaking, quoting (dialect?). Important: inconspicuous, attitude, subskills before complex tasks, check out school resources, models.

Source: Francis P. Robinson, *Effective Reading* (New York: Harper & Row, Publishers, 1962).

these is outline form. Since most teachers follow an outline when they lecture, students can develop an intuitive understanding of outlining by taking notes on an organized lecture. Teachers might even list the main points to be covered on the board or on an overhead projector, explaining that each main point will contain several subpoints and each subpoint will be illustrated, and showing how this is written.

Outline form, of course, is a hierarchically organized list of main points and subpoints:

I. Main points are listed in numerical order using Roman numerals.
  A. Subpoints are listed and indented under each main point.
  B. Each subpoint is listed using capital letters.
    1. Examples illustrating the subpoints may be listed and indented further under each subpoint.
    2. Examples use Arabic numbers.

Outlines are made up either of sentences or of phrases. They are organized by two principles: first, each item in a parallel line (with the same kind of number or letter and at the same indentation from the margin) must be just as general as every other item on that line. Second, items must become more specific as they move to the right in their indentation.

Outlines can also be made from written texts. Indeed, the more experience students have with retrieving outlines from lectures and texts, the more they internalize the hierarchical pattern. A word of caution, however: retrieving somebody else's outline is not the same thing as constructing an outline of one's own. In the case of lectures and written texts, the categories are already established and the original outline, already written by the author or teacher, only has to be derived and reconstructed by the student. By way of contrast, when students must construct their own outlines from information they have gathered, the categories are not supplied. It is when naming the categories and articulating the generalizations that students come to discover what they mean to say. That, incidentally, is why it is sometimes wrong to *begin* a complex project with an outline, although an outline may eventually emerge once material is gathered and categorized.

Problems with outline form come when students are unable to identify levels of generality or relationships among different sets of data. Therefore, outlining can't really be taught as a form; it must be taught as a method of categorizing. Generally categorizing is best taught by the manipulation of materials, such as chemicals or objects. It can also be taught on the abstract level with individual words or sentences. Figure 4.2 represents a list of objects which could be manipulated into three groups, the groups labeled, and the labels written down as main points in an outline. Similarly, Figure 4.3 represents a list of sentences (minus the "topic sentences" which would express their commonality) that could be manipulated into three groups and then into an outline.

Figure 4.2 requires labeling and Figure 4.3 requires topic sentences before the data can be written as an outline. One of the most misunderstood aspects of outlining is that the categories or main headings need to be invented. That is why students cannot learn outlining simply by making an outline of somebody else's chapter or lecture.

The point here is that even though lectures often proceed from outlines made by the teacher and often result in notes taken by students in outline form, the process of taking notes may not in itself teach students how to make their own outlines. Nor can a teacher assume that lecturing from an outline guarantees that students are perceiving and recording the hierarchical relationships among data. Some inductive method of teaching categorization might need to precede notetaking. Collecting notes after a lecture or assessing general ability to categorize (as suggested in Chapter 3) might reveal which students need work on these organizing skills.

HELPING STUDENTS TAKE GOOD NOTES

A variation on outline form is to forget about Roman numerals and the use of letters or numbers, concentrating instead on taking notes in phrases (instead of sentences) and grouping information in clumps so that relationships among individual facts are clear. Some general guidelines for this fairly natural system of notetaking are shown in Figure 4.4. Figure 4.5 shows an example of notes following these guidelines.

FIGURE 4.2

CATEGORIZATION EXERCISE

DIVIDE UP THE MATERIALS LIST BELOW IN TWO WAYS:

1. List the materials under these headings: *Elements, Compounds,* and *Mixtures.*
2. Then list the same materials under these headings: *Liquids, Solids,* and *Gases.*

List of Materials

alcohol	calcium	methane	sodium chloride
asphalt	petroleum	helium	polonium
copper	lead	pitchblende	radium
lithium	phosphorus	potash	ink
cesium	titanium	lime	copper oxide

Source: Based on an exercise in Judith Bechtel and Bettie Franzblau, *Reading in the Science Classroom* (Washington, D.C.: National Education Association, 1980), 42.

FIGURE 4.3
_____

FACTS TO BE ORGANIZED INTO AN OUTLINE

DIRECTIONS:
Decide what some of these sentences have in common with one another. Sentences which have something in common should be grouped together and listed under a sentence which explains what they have in common. That sentence will be their heading in an outline. In other words, you are being given the items A, B, C, etc. for an outline. You have to come up with the Roman numerals I, II, III. The sentences as written here may not be in the order that you will want for your outline.

1. Boston mobs hauled William Lloyd Garrison, an abolitionist, through the street with a rope around his waist in the 1850s.
2. The Reverend Jonathan Mayhew, a Puritan minister in the early mid-1700s, called the Church of Rome "a filthy prostitute."
3. At one time or another each one of the thirteen colonies disenfranchised Catholics.
4. In 1819 in Belleville, Illinois, Timothy Bennett was hanged for killing his neighbor in a rifle duel at twenty-five paces.
5. In Wisconsin one member of the legislature shot a fellow member dead on the floor of the house during the early days.
6. One of the last formal duels was fought in 1877 between James Gordon Bennett, Jr., and the brother of a woman he was supposed to have insulted.
7. A mob of anti-abolitionists set fire to a brand-new hall in Philadelphia when abolitionists held a convention there.
8. Mobs in Cincinnati broke up an abolitionist's printing press and burned the homes of some blacks.
9. In 1831 in New York City inflammatory public lectures about the Pope were common.

Answers:
   I. The early colonies had a history of anti-Catholicism. (Items 2, 3, 9)
  II. In various cities mobs did violence against abolitionists. (Items 1, 7, 8)
 III. Duels were still staged in the 1800s. (Items 4, 5, 6)

Source: Based on J.C. Furnas, The Americans: A Social History of the United States 1587–1914 (New York: G.P. Putnam, 1969).

_____

Another system of taking notes is called the Cornell System.[4] The Cornell format for notetaking allows the writer to interpret and organize material while taking notes. Using "law-ruled" paper or drawing a vertical line about one-fourth of the way across the page from the left edge, the writer takes notes to the right of this line and writes key terms for recitation, reflection, and review to the left of it. The writer's interpretations are thus clearly distinguished from the content material. This format encourages active and ongoing responses to the new material. Figure 4.6 illustrates the Cornell format.

A useful instructional method is to model good notetaking. Invite a guest lecturer to speak and record what is said on overhead transparencies. Compare your notes and your students' notes afterwards.

FIGURE 4.4

GUIDELINES FOR GOOD NOTES*

1. *Always label and date your notes.* For class, labeling means writing the topic, whether or not it is announced. For readings, labeling means chapters, pages, or source (if other than the textbook).
2. *Take notes that look more like lists than paragraphs.* Discrete pieces of information will be easier to find.
3. *Space notes so that related bits of information are visibly together and separated from other related bits.* Outline form does this best, but simply skipping a line when the topic changes can have the same effect. Organizing notes this way helps with interpreting the information, selecting what is important and why.
4. *Write down more than the main ideas.* Include enough details, facts, or examples that you will be able to understand the main ideas later and be able to use them for projects, tests, etc.
5. *Use phrases and abbreviations, but be clear enough that you will later be able to read what you've written.* Try to compress the information in a way that would be clear to a classmate, but not necessarily clear to a stranger.
6. *Be neat enough that re-copying is not necessary.* There are better uses for study time.
7. *Devise a system for reacting as you go.* In the margins or with a special system of marking private thoughts, write your questions, comments, or applications about the information you are taking notes on. These reactions will be handy for discussion and review.
8. *Create signals to mark important things.* Use stars, underlining, arrows, or other symbols to code the special parts of your notes.

*Should include also any special considerations that apply to a particular course or a particular task.

FIGURE 4.5

SAMPLE NOTES

FIGURE 4.5 (continued)

SAMPLE NOTES

② Length of light
can be accurate to 1 part in 10^9
on interferometer
(apparently not ever adapted)

★ ③ Atomic standard
meter : 1, 650, 763. 73 wavelengths
of orange-red radiation
$2P_{10} - 5d_5$
emitted by an isotope of Krypton Kr^{86}
Advantage :
    a) accurate
    b) available

Source: Based on Robert Resnick and David Halliday, *Physics, Part I*, 3rd ed. (New York: John Wiley & Sons, Inc., 1977), 6–7.

FIGURE 4.6

SAMPLE NOTES TAKEN USING THE CORNELL FORMAT

9/21 Employment Problems

Key terms | unemployment – wants to work, but can't find job
underemployment – includes unemployed plus those working full-time for very low wages;

FIGURE 4.6 (continued)

SAMPLE NOTES TAKEN USING THE CORNELL FORMAT

	working part-time, but wanting full-time, others missed on surveys
Job traits	*unstructured — no job ladders, no clear work relationships, no job variety, low wages*
Characteristics of people	*underdeveloped skills, unpredictable patterns of work*
Statistics	*by mid 70's — 50–60% of urban black population underemployed vs. 15% unemployed*
Orthodox analysis	*low productivity = low wages*

Source: Based on David M. Gordon. *Problems in Political Economy: An Urban Perspective,* Second Edition. Copyright© 1977 by D.C. Heath and Company, pp. 53–58. Used with permission of the publisher.

SELECTIVE NOTETAKING

Any one system of notetaking loses its effectiveness when students become bored with it. A more challenging task than taking notes, although one which involves extra planning by the teacher, is to offer some graphic representation of the concepts which alert students to the relationships among pieces of information. These are referred to as "Advance Organizers," a term invented by David P. Ausubel.[5] The teacher provides the structure, and the student's job is to fill in specific words and phrases as they fit. Figure 4.7 is an example of an Advance Organizer. The idea is to capture the important relationships visually.

FIGURE 4.7

SAMPLE ADVANCE ORGANIZER

DIRECTIONS:
In this section of the textbook you will read about many separate experiments. Each illustrates some aspect of Anderson's metaphor for how the mind works: a Superordinate Executive System makes use of various Subordinate Systems to delegate parts of complex tasks. Your job is to make a chart which reflects this hierarchical structure. Identify as many Subordinate Systems as you can, naming the tasks relegated to them in the various experiments mentioned. Some parts of the Subordinate Systems are named for you as examples.

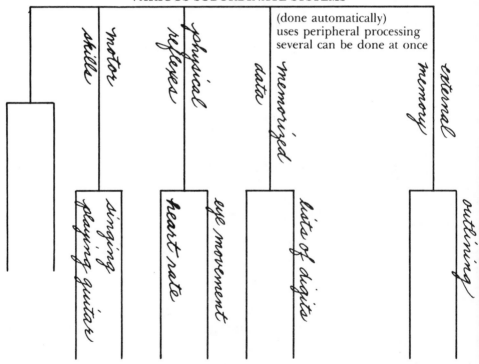

THE SUPERORDINATE EXECUTIVE SYSTEM

(conscious intention)
employs goals
uses central serial processing

VARIOUS SUBORDINATE SYSTEMS

(done automatically)
uses peripheral processing
several can be done at once

motor skills

physical reflexes

memorized data

external memory

singing playing guitar

heart rate

eye movement

lists of digits

outlining

Source: Based on Barry F. Anderson, *Cognitive Psychology: The Study of Knowing, Learning, and Thinking* (New York: Academic Press, 1975), 152–174.

Students can then sort out relevant from irrelevant information as they read a chapter, hear a lecture, or participate in some other activity. Figure 4.8 shows some of the other shapes that can be adapted when using Advance Organizers for selective notetaking.

Another form of selective notetaking involves enticing students into some special focus for a chapter. For example, students can

FIGURE 4.8

SHAPES THAT CAN BE USED FOR ADVANCE ORGANIZERS

PIES

The whole and its parts show proportions.

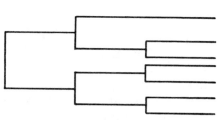

HIERARCHIES

The branches show subcategories and examples.

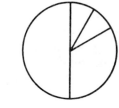

SPOKES

The hub depicts a main idea, and the spokes represent details when all details are of equal importance.

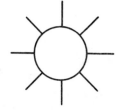

FLOW CHARTS

The geometric shapes represent stages and the arrows indicate the direction taken by main idea, subordinate idea, and details.

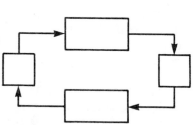

Source: Used with permission from Judith Bechtel and Bettie Franzblau, *Reading in the Science Classroom* (Washington, D.C.: National Education Association, 1980), 40.

be asked to list practical problems raised in a certain chapter. Or the teacher can present students with a problem or question before assigning the reading. Then their job is to record such data as would contribute evidence to a persuasive answer (which can, incidentally, be used later on an essay test). For example, in chemistry class the teacher could ask students to keep track of all aspects of gas laws which could have practical applications in their homes. Or students of literature could be asked to survey members of their family on how they picture hell before reading Dante's *Inferno*, and then record the similarities or differences they find between their family members' image and those in the text.

To structure the notetaking for a particularly difficult reading assignment, teachers may want to make up study guides. Study guides are usually prepared to direct students' attention to three levels of comprehension: the literal level (facts), the interpretive level (understanding of facts in relationship), and application (understanding the concepts implicit in the facts). Figure 4.9 represents such a study guide.

DEVELOPING THE HABIT OF QUESTIONING

Better than teacher-made study guides, however, are student-made study guides. Students who know how to form questions are actively engaged in inquiry and will better understand what they read and hear.

Students should write questions as *part* of their informal or expressive writing and as part of their notetaking. However, before good questions become an ongoing part of the class activities, some instruction in questioning technique will probably be necessary. Figure 4.10 lists some of the different kinds of questions students have to become familiar with. At first students will ask only factual questions, and it will take considerable practice before they move into higher-order questions. It will take even longer before the questions are *real* questions as opposed to mere exercises in questioning. Students could be given a handout similar to Figure 4.10 and then encouraged to practice questioning in ways that build on writing or culminate in a writing task. For example:

- Have the class brainstorm questions in response to a lecture, activity or class reading assignment (aiming quickly for quantity, building on previous questions, not pre-judging the questions); then categorize the questions or rank order them according to the kinds of questions listed in Figure 4.10.
- Let students categorize and label the questions in their textbooks according to the list in Figure 4.10.

FIGURE 4.9

SAMPLE STUDY GUIDE

Note: Study Guides should progress from the *literal understanding* of vocabulary and facts through *interpretation* to *application* of the material.

I. Be able to explain the following in your own words:
  A. "Lower" organisms than ourselves.
  B. "A single cross," as in the second line of the second paragraph.
  C. "Marks on human faces" as in the middle of the third paragraph.
  D. What Mendel did in his experiments to study heredity.
  E. Which relatives of yours could be included in a study to trace hereditary traits in human beings.

II. Jot down your reasons for choosing the most likely answer to each of the following questions:
  A. Pick the most likely range of years considered to represent a human generation:
    1. 40–50 years
    2. 5–7 years
    3. 10–20 years
    4. 100–200 years
  B. (True or false) A good way to study the influence of environment on human genetics is to study identical twins.
  C. The picture at the top of the page is supposed to show:
    1. that sunlight causes people to squint.
    2. that people can't communicate very well.
    3. that hairstyles change.
    4. that members of the same family look alike.
III. Write out brief answers to the following problems:
  A. We often hear about experiments performed on rats to determine whether different things cause cancer in humans. Which of the reasons given for studying heredity in drosophila seem to be good reasons for studying cancer in rats?
  B. Someone has suggested that you do a study on heredity using one of the following animals: elephants, sponges, or mosquitoes. Which do you think would be most useful? Which least useful? Why?
  C. Why would you consider any of these statements to be possible or impossible?
    1. Two brown-eyed parents could produce a blue-eyed baby.
    2. You could find another person who had exactly your same genetic makeup if you had the time to check out every single living person on earth.
    3. You could change your genes by changing your diet.
    4. Human beings in the future will be producing more offspring than at present.

Source: Some of these questions were taken from Judith Bechtel and Bettie Franzblau, *Reading in the Science Classroom* (Washington, D.C.: National Education Association, 1980), 33–36. All are based on James H. Otto and Albert Towle, *Modern Biology* (New York: Holt, Rinehart & Winston, 1977), 127–128.

- Tape record a genuine question and answer period; then analyze the questions according to Figure 4.9.
- Assign students to bring in ten questions a week for homework.
- Make a chart, similar to the list in Figure 4.9, and have a student record numbers or examples of each type of question.

FIGURE 4.10

KINDS OF QUESTIONS

    I. Knowledge Questions: recall of fact
       e.g.: 1. What does the symbol stand for?
            2. Who was President of the U.S. when the Civil War started?
    II. Comprehension Questions: translation of data into another form
       e.g.: 1. Why does litmus paper change color?
            2. How were the peace settlements after World War II different from
         the Treaty of Versailles?
  III. Application Questions: using general principles in a new context
       e.g.: 1. On this map (any topographical map without cities), where would
         you expect to find a city? Why?
            2. If you filled the gas tank at 15,000 miles and then put in 15 more gallons
         at 15,300 miles, how many miles did you get to the gallon of gasoline?
  IV. Analysis Questions: ability to separate complex problems into their component
     parts
       e.g.: 1. On what basis are plants classified into their various phyla?
            2. How is variety introduced into Bartok's "Concerto for Orchestra"?
    V. Evaluation Questions: making judgments according to some criteria
       e.g.: 1. Which description of the mole concept in chemistry would be most appro-
         priate for a sixth grader and why?
            2. What is the best argument for capital punishment and what is the
         worst? Why do you select these particular arguments?

Source: Based on Francis P. Hunkins, *Involving Students in Questioning* (Boston: Allyn and Bacon, 1976), 29–66.

- Identify problems with the questions that have been generated in these ways and suggest improvements that could be made.

Incidentally, an obvious advantage of teaching questioning is that the students use their own questions and thus contribute more to their own learning than is the case when students answer ready-made questions set up by the teacher or the textbook company. The best student-generated questions can be used on tests in addition to substituting for official study guides.

INFORMAL OR EXPRESSIVE WRITING AGAIN

Another form of record-keeping is more personal and private than notes or questions. This form is a record of personal reactions to the materials of the course, including the class activities. Students may keep journals, recording observations, opinions, disagreements, questions, and speculations about what they read or hear in class. New material, after all, is not merely added to old when new information is learned. The old itself must sometimes be modified. Therefore, some type of speculative "thinking on paper" should accompany factual notetaking. In this way students can be pushed to move from fact through classification to speculation and theory (where true assimilation occurs). Accordingly, the individual entries in journals should be at least one page long—or twenty minutes' worth of fast writing—since insights come only after the obvious has been written down and associations pushed. Short entries will usually record only the most obvious, general points.

Some type of expressive writing should be a part of all content courses. These writings represent the ultimate in individualizing assignments since each student will interpret the challenges in his or her own way.

In order to build in some opportunities for students to reflect and become conscious of changes in their understanding of course material, they should make a table of contents for their journal entries, listing those entries which are significant because of the comparisons or insights developed in them.[6] Even better would be for each student to prepare a preface to the journal after making the table of contents. In the preface students would summarize the uses they made of their journal as well as changes they recorded in their understanding of material. Such an activity would serve a very important educational function: it would help students recognize their own accomplishments. The journal record serves this invaluable function whenever it demonstrates the sudden attainment of a concept (sometimes called the "Aha!" experience). Once that occurs, the previous state of innocence about that set of data is almost impossible to recapture; hence the record of the change is invaluable.

If journals are kept, they should be graded on quantity and not read to be corrected. Comments should never be critical of how things are expressed. In order to encourage perfect freedom and lack of fear concerning these informal writings, all responses to them—whether by teachers or by peers—should be deliberately supportive and context-specific. Figure 4.11 represents a typical journal entry with appropriate responses written in the margin. Actually teachers need not read these journals in their entirety. Students might, however, voluntarily share parts of what they have written.

PROCESS LOGS

When students are responsible for a complicated task, such as completing a lab experiment or writing a research paper, they might learn a great deal by keeping a process log. This is a structured list of time spent, equipment used, and stages of participation experienced on a

FIGURE 4.11

TYPICAL JOURNAL ENTRY WITH APPROPRIATE RESPONSES

6/2/84 Jazz.

    The basic notes of jazz are very versitile. That's why many forms of jazz branched off from it. Blues are really a slower version of jazz. Rock has links with jazz also. In jazz you can take a basic sound and do a lot with it. You can weave all around that sound in various rhythmic patterns, The basis [sic] sound being the Harmonic Vocabulary.

What i
the lin
betwee
rock ar
jazz?

Have you played in a jazz group yourself?

6/3/84 Tension

    I have heard what we have discussed in music. I've heard the tension release in action but never realized how import [sic] the first and last notes are. It really sounds bad if you don't put that final note of release after building up tension. It makes me more aware of the effect that music really has on us as listeners.

Can you think of advertisements or movies which make use of tension/release for certain effects?

Source: From the Music Appreciation Class of Gary Johnston, Northern Kentucky University.

---

project. Part of the satisfaction derived from a process log comes from the design of the record. Another part of the satisfaction comes from the self-insights gained from sharing patterns among students and across tasks. Habits and dispositions become definable, and learning is seen as dynamic rather than static, the individual student being free to choose from among different ways of approaching a task. Insights include better ways of proceeding next time.

INDEPENDENT STUDY

Whenever coursework is individualized, notetaking and record-keeping become even more important. Process logs, lists of resources consulted, notes, and journals should always be a part of any independent study undertaken by groups of students or by individual students. Expressive responses written regularly are also very important as an ongoing part of such projects. Even if the independent study is to be concretely evident (e.g., a science fair project, a skit, a report), more will be learned when record-keeping is part of the process. Furthermore, if the result of the project is to take written shape, the final manuscript will seem a much less formidable task if it can be built from earlier writings.

Students will flounder less and have more of a sense of direction about their work if they keep records as they go. If the project is not working out well or if some changes of focus need to be renegotiated, writing will help bring these problems to light. Independent study projects are thus easier to supervise and evaluate when ongoing record-keeping is specified and checked in-process rather than merely collected at the end. This regulatory function is a crucial factor if one teacher is supervising several such projects or a whole class of independent study at the same time.

SMALL GROUP WORK

Good teaching allows students time to verbalize their understanding of the material. It only makes sense that this should be done in small groups where each student would get more chance to participate. Whole classes, by contrast, are likely to be dominated by just a few students, with the direction of the discussion determined by the first few participants, leaving many other viewpoints unexamined. Small group work is particularly appropriate when concepts are difficult, issues are controversial, or applications are complex.

Small groups work especially well when a writing task has preceded the group work. The writing focuses attention and records a kind of commitment to the task at hand so that the group doesn't have to start from scratch. Chapter 2 contains a fuller explanation of the care that should be taken in preparing students for group work. In general, students must be assured of a business-like, but supportive atmosphere and have models for responding to each other's work before they can be expected to get real work done. Their earliest tasks should be specific, structured, and as little value-laden as possible. Once these dynamics have been considered, myriads of uses for small groups come to mind:

- Sharing journal responses to a particularly difficult chapter, story, or poem, singling out the most interesting sentences from each, and then selecting one to report to the whole class.
- Working from a set of three discrete facts to come up with a conclusion or "topic sentence," a generalization that would tie together all three facts. This activity would be very similar to the one described in Figure 4.3 as an exercise to teach outlining.
- Inventing questions over a reading assignment or a lecture, using as many different question types as are listed in Figure 4.10.
- Deciding on the best answers to an Advance Organizer or Study Guide. Inappropriate answers will be explained by members of the group, thus relieving the beleaguered teacher of some drudgery.

It is often advisable to build into group work some additional record-keeping functions. The group should write down its accomplishments, especially if these will prove useful to the rest of the class or contribute to an ongoing project. Highlights from these records can then be shared briefly (thus providing practice with summarizing) with the whole class. The "reporting back" function of small groups is important, since students need training in listening to each other and also need guidance in talking to each other. Most students will report back to the teacher rather than to the class, out of habit. They need to consider their audience, selecting only what would be interesting or useful to the rest of the class.

WHAT RECORD-KEEPING LEADS TO

Of course the ultimate project involving record-keeping is the report or research paper. Whatever the resources used—whether library materials, careful observation, or personal interview—record-keeping needs to precede the actual drafting of the paper. The demands of such complex tasks will obviously seem much less forbidding if record-keeping has been a regular part of the rest of the coursework.

The more immediate payoff for good record-keeping is improved performance on tests. Students who keep good records do better on tests because they have paid more attention as they listened, read, and participated; also because they have rehearsed their knowledge by writing it down. Furthermore, by casting things into their own words, students make it their own. And if they keep their notes, they have a permanent aid to recollection and a record of achievement.

Occasionally teachers ask how they can motivate their students to like writing, to think of it as important. Many times students return after they are older and more experienced to say that they *now* know how important writing is. Testimonials to that effect from returning students or professionals in the field do sometimes convince younger students to look at writing skill in a new way. But the most convincing arguments in favor of using writing to learn are those based in the here and now: young students gaining a sense of control over course material through writing. Good record-keeping provides its own rewards.

NOTES

1. Barry F. Anderson, *Cognitive Psychology: The Study of Knowing, Learning, and Thinking* (New York: Academic Press, 1975), 159.

2. Research conducted at South Lakes High School, Fairfax County, Virginia, by Anne Miller Wottring, reported at a workshop entitled "Talking and Writing Across the Curriculum: Theory-based Practice," National Convention of the National Council of Teachers of English, Washington, D.C., November, 1980.

3. Francis P. Robinson, *Effective Reading* (New York: Harper & Row, Publishers, 1962).

4. Walter Pauk, *How to Study in College* (Boston: Houghton Mifflin Co., 1974).

5. David P. Ausubel, "The Use of Advance Organizers in the Learning and Retention of Meaningful Verbal Material," *Journal of Educational Psychology* 51 (October 1960): 267–274.

6. I learned to use journals in this way from Toby Fulwiler at a Faculty Workshop, "Writing Across the Disciplines," sponsored by the National Endowment for the Humanities at Northern Kentucky University, Highland Heights, Kentucky, May, 1981. Fulwiler credits the idea to Dixie Goswami at the NEH Seminar "Writing in the Learning of Humanities," Rutgers University, New Brunswick, New Jersey, July, 1977.

5

Research Papers

Research papers are assigned so frequently because they represent the whole learning process in miniature. Students are motivated by some question or discrepancy in information, they find out what information is available, they research this information, they form a hypothesis, they muster parts of their new-found information to support the hypothesis, and they write what they have found, documenting the sources. Thus the student has pursued some problem of personal interest independently, assimilated the information, and communicated it.

For the purposes of this chapter we will assume that research papers involve incorporation of information from outside sources into a piece of writing. Normally these papers follow a prescribed format. They have an introduction, main body, and conclusion, and maintain an objective, formal tone. The length can be as short as one page. The reliance on outside information can vary from use of outside sources in subordination of a personal idea to the simple rearrangement of information from a single source. In all cases the writer is assumed to be in control of the selection of what to include and the ordering of information, but the extent of personal comment and the kind of format used may vary from assignment to assignment. In no case, however, does copying—or using strings of copied material—substitute for research. The emphasis is on integration of information, not merely on transmitting it. In short, the writer is the mediator, not merely the finder and reporter of data.

SUBVERSIONS OF THE RESEARCH PROCESS

At the highest level we would call well-done research a dissertation, and all good research projects are, in a sense, miniature dissertations. The problem is that this idealized version of the process is not what many students do. Typically, students are assigned a topic, they put off researching it as long as possible, they finally find one source which can be summarized or copied, they use encyclopedias or the card catalogue to gain enough other sources for reference as may be required for specific citations and bibliography, and they write all this up haltingly in what approximates the prescribed form. Not only do students frequently compose outlines after the paper is written, but notecards (when required) as well. Often this parody of the research process teaches students little, fails to familiarize them with the resources available, and hardens their attitudes against writing in general.

At the other extreme are students who work long hours, painstakingly recording every detail from every source they consult, compiling a massive accumulation of data, often meticulously transcribing all that they find. Such students have not learned to select, subordinate, or summarize. Their writing lacks control; their time use is inefficient. They have been overwhelmed by the task and have responded to it by hoping that their monumental efforts will be rewarded. Then, if their research papers do not receive high grades, they become unduly discouraged, wrongly assuming that they should not try so hard the next time.

Quite naturally the teacher assigning research papers is equally discouraged, partly because of the students' lost opportunities for learning, partly out of frustration that students seem so ill prepared to accomplish this kind of task, and partly because of all the work involved in grading such projects. If the teacher were to "walk the students" through the whole process, the frustration level of both teacher and students might be higher yet because it is boring to hear about processes that can only be understood and appreciated as they develop. Nothing is harder to follow, for example, than an explanation of how to use a periodical index before you have actually tried. It is a little like teaching people the motions of swimming before they have been in the water. If the teacher's role includes merely designing instructions for the assignment of a research paper and then later evaluating the written product, the process is very likely to be subverted.

Subversion of a research project may take the form of an unsatisfying process or it may take the form of actual cheating. The dividing line between incompetence and cheating is hard to define. On the one hand, there are businesses willing to sell students finished research papers on a variety of topics and levels of difficulty. On the other hand, there are teachers who encourage their students to copy texts for reports because the information is deemed to be the important thing, not the language skills required for summarizing. Little do these teachers realize that learning comes from the process of selecting and translating information, and, further, that any gaps or mistakes in the "translation" should be welcomed as the beginning of new learning! Other subverters of the research process include friends and relatives who do most of the work of a research paper in the name of helping students to succeed. In short, research projects, which should be among the most pleasurable learning experiences a student has, seem instead to bring out the worst in people.

The teacher is faced with several choices in response to this subversion:

1. Ignore the trouble spots and continue to expect honest, well-done research papers.
2. Assume the role of investigator and punish those caught cheating.
3. Rethink research assignments to maximize learning and minimize frustration.

The special emphasis of this chapter is on the third of these options.

IMPROVING ASSIGNMENTS

Research papers are a microcosm of the learning process. They also involve the most complex skills of any intellectual activity. The whole process of skimming vast amounts of material, selecting what is relevant, and subordinating this information to an organizational plan of one's own is terribly complex. And this does not account for the more routine sub-skills of locating materials in a library or knowing how to use direct quotations. In addition, the whole question of motivation and self-concept affects the learning process. Students will not take naturally to research projects if their family or significant peers do not value independence, their school atmosphere is not intellectually stimulating, or their classroom does not encourage open-ended questioning. Nor will they understand what is required if they never have the opportunity to read finished research papers written by other students of their own age and ability. In short, research writing involves sustained, complicated effort, and it involves social behaviors as well as intellectual skills.

In designing research projects, then, the teacher should be conscious of the many variables that affect the writing process. Always the teacher must be conscious of having options to choose from in assigning research tasks, using class time for instruction in writing, and varying the evaluation procedures. Varying the usual way these things are handled does not necessarily mean a "lowering of standards" or a change in ultimate expectations as to what students should be accomplishing in the long run. Preparing students to eventually do formal, critical papers does not necessarily mean doing them over and over again at earlier and earlier ages. Instead, teachers should plan the learning they want to come from the research project and rest secure in their understanding that certain changes in the way the assignment is handled can have very far-reaching effects.

Minor changes in the research assignment, for example, might give students badly needed experience with one sub-skill by minimizing the other constraints. Changes which enhance motivation spark more commitment to the task and hence better papers. For instance, a student who interviews her grandmother as part of a civics paper on the Great Depression will take more pride in her library research on that topic than she would if she saw no connection between herself and the 1930s. Similarly, a student of American literature will take more pride in composing a documentary script on Edgar Allen Poe's life than he or she would in trying to summarize reviews of Poe's work by literary critics or biographers.

There are many ways to promote "ownership" or pride in research papers, better attitudes toward the research process, and more successful papers. Generally one must bridge the gap between the students' earlier experience with research projects and the kind of abstract ideal normally associated with such tasks. The following variables are meant to be suggestive as bridge-builders:

1. Topics should be appropriately specified so that the task will be manageable, but not stifling.
2. When the topic and resources are close to the students' experience and the rest of the coursework, students have a greater personal stake in the project.
3. Experimenting with purpose and audience for research papers is preferable to always expecting formal academic prose.
4. Earlier intervention in the writing process is preferable to extensive correction of the final paper.
5. Several shorter research papers are preferable to one long paper for inexperienced writers.

Some of the specific suggestions made below will show how to adapt these general principles.

THE COMPLEXITY OF THE TASK

In order to design good research tasks teachers must also be aware of the complexity of the writing skills necessary for such tasks. In fact, one reason for manipulating the variables of traditional research tasks is to allow students some "comfort zones," that is, to allow them to get used to a few new expectations at a time. Thus writing an abstract or summary of one source to share with a group may teach documentation skills without taxing the student's ability to organize multiple sources. In choosing which variable to manipulate teachers will want to keep their initial assessment of student abilities in mind. Teachers also should remember that research papers require all of the following skills:

1. Locating materials
2. Taking notes
3. Summarizing
4. Organizing a vast body of information
5. Using quotations and documenting correctly
6. Mastering the format
7. Revising and editing

Each of these skills will be discussed more fully.

Finding Resources

Research writing commonly involves use of reference books, periodical indexes, and the card catalog in the library. Becoming familiar with these resources may be the main goal of a research project—for future reference. In other words, the focus of the assignment could be awareness of how to find things. If so, students should be encouraged to seek help from librarians, especially at unfamiliar libraries. Sometimes a writer's problem is not being able to find materials, but more often it is the opposite: being overwhelmed with a surfeit of information. Part of the library experience, therefore, should entail making judgments about the appropriateness of material for a certain task.

Probably the most common mistake made by teachers in regard to using resources is to encourage the use of encyclopedias and other already synthesized references. It is very difficult for students to judge the appropriateness of the information in encyclopedias and hence to choose from among the bits of information already synthesized there. The authors and editors have already pruned inessential information, and students find very little to leave out when they summarize. Therefore, they end up copying rather than controlling what they write. Inexperienced students also have difficulty using literary criticism, abstract analyses of the lives and works of poets and writers. For one thing, most secondary students are unable to evaluate the validity of abstract interpretations. At least one authority insists that better papers and better learning come when students work with lower-order documents (e.g., first-hand accounts, diaries, cases, profiles). According to James Moffett,

Original research with higher-order documents is of course not impossible, but unless one is an authority in a subject area, the likelihood of originality . . . decreases as the abstraction level of the sources rises.[1]

Synthesized sources are not easy for students to use, and they are not innately interesting to inexperienced writers. Of more interest are materials that touch the students' lives or excite their imaginations. Figure 5.1 illustrates the various resources that could be drawn upon for research papers and how far removed they are from the students' own experience.

In general it is better for inexperienced writers to use sources closer to the first-hand experience of the self, creating meanings from these, rather than to rely on the abstractions of more far-removed library sources.

At any rate, the teacher should be aware that locating materials is quite a distinct concern from the writing skills involved. Minimizing problems here could allow emphasis on other, more essential components of research paper writing. Conversely, locating materials could be an end in itself, quite properly isolated from the more difficult intellectual strategies involved in a research project.

When the research task is defined in a larger sense, teachers may see that research need not be limited to library materials. Careful observation, interviewing, and even experimenting can and should be incorporated into the research task, whenever possible, as a means of personalizing the writing and expanding the student's opportunities for integrating diverse materials.

Taking Notes

In taking notes students transpose information into their own words. Thus they are condensing, sifting, and interpreting. Unfortunately, the ever-present copy machines have eliminated the absolute physical necessity of taking notes, encouraging instead a kind of "pastiche" approach to using multiple sources. Few students realize that direct quotations should be copied (and marked as direct quotations) *only* when the wording is so clever that a paraphrase would ruin it. Having a purpose other than conveying information (i.e., solving a problem, applying knowledge to a specific case, etc.) makes the taking of notes more purposeful. Then it becomes clear why individual notecards are recommended: that way discrete bits of information from various sources can be rearranged in different combinations. This ability to control resource material is the purpose of notetaking, a skill that cannot be expected on research projects if it is not encouraged for other purposes in a given course.

FIGURE 5.1

THE RELATIONSHIP OF RESEARCH SOURCES TO THE EXPERIENCES OF THE STUDENT

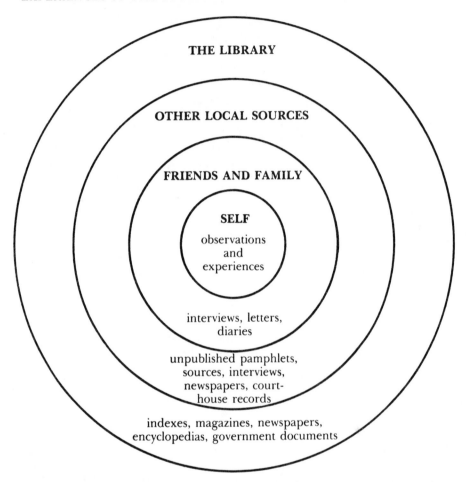

Source: Adapted by Frances Zaniello, Northern Kentucky University, from a lecture by Gordon Pradl, New York University.

Ability to Summarize

Of primary importance in writing a research paper is the need to digest material and transpose it into one's own words. Summaries are shortened versions of some outside resource, most commonly a book or article. To summarize, students must be able to understand the material and then to identify main points. Finally, summarizing involves the ability to distinguish between materials in a resource which are relevant to an outside consideration (i.e., the thesis or purpose of a particular research study) and those which are not. Thus a student researching space satellites must be able to read through an article on weather forecasting, for example, and summarize from it only those points relevant to the topic. The twin abilities of sorting and reconstructing so central to summarizing must be developed prior to a research assignment.

Organizing a Vast Body of Information

Contrary to student opinion, the problem in doing research papers is not how to make the paper long enough, but how to bring all the potential information under control. One aspect of this control, of course, is the discovery and articulation of a particular slant or thesis. By definition, research papers in their final form are organized. Rarely is a research paper written in narrative form where the chronological order of happenings serves as an organizational principle. Teachers, wishing to minimize the organizational demands of research writing, however, might do well to realize that a narrative plan is the easiest for inexperienced writers to organize.

All the while students are selecting and condensing information in notes, they are organizing. People differ in their need to have a plan or special slant prior to beginning to write. Very often an outline and even a decision about the main point or thesis of a research paper emerges midway through the writing or even *after* the preliminary draft is completed. This may necessitate a change in the original order of presentation, if not in the main point to be emphasized.

Teachers need to be aware of how hard it is for students enmeshed in content to stand back, look at their work objectively for form, and see the readers' expectations of a presentation which packs all the information about one sub-point into a single section of the paper, no matter that the information came from various sources. It is difficult for inexperienced writers to make the conscious choice of building sub-points into each other in a logical progression. The more complex the topic, the harder it is to outline. Here is where small groups on revising could be of immense help. (See suggestions later in this chapter for small group work on revising.)

Proper outlining and even paragraphing cannot be assumed if students have had very little practice at seeing relationships and articulating them. Until these skills are a natural part of less intimidating or smaller tasks, they cannot be depended on for research writing where so many other skills are brought to bear.

Mastering the Format

Convention and convenience normally dictate the format of research papers. Convention dictates the rules of quoting as well as the citation and bibliographic forms. Convenience dictates the need for documentation: the reader of a research paper might want to refer again to the sources for further reference. It is important for teachers to mention these factors of convention and convenience because otherwise research formats seem very arbitrary. Students need to know that there are variations in the form; otherwise they are very confused by seeming contradictions in the demands of different teachers. They need to know, too, that adherence to *some* definite form is a prerequisite for members of an academic community. Thus different disciplines have different documentation methods to meet the particular demands of researchers in that discipline.

Whatever the format expectations, students need to see actual papers written according to these expectations. Directions, no matter how clear, do not provide enough information to the novice about how a variety of topics would be appropriately poured into a given format. Also, students cannot know how convenient the format is for readers unless they have been in the role of reader where other papers are concerned. Most important of all, examples of research papers provide students with a feel for the tone and formality of a research project. By reading model papers students sense the whole point of the research project on more levels than when told of this or that.

What makes research papers so difficult for inexperienced writers may not be the format so much as the reason for the format. Most students are simply unfamiliar with the scholar's role. A research paper writer is, in a sense, playing the role of scholar. He or she is not merely reporting an intellectual quest, mustering evidence for what amounts to a theoretical position, but also assuming the role of expert. The formal tone and slang-free diction are more like textbook writing than like what students may be used to writing in other contexts. Teachers, more used to academic prose, are sometimes unaware of the alienation young students feel from such a context. Given the other problems attendant to composing an extended piece of writing using outside sources, teachers may want to vary the research activity in such a way as to minimize the formality of tone.

Not only is the role of scholar-as-writer unfamiliar, but the audience of scholars-as-readers (for which the teacher usually stands in proxy) is also unfamiliar. To dramatize the role of critical readers for research projects, teachers may wish to look beyond the classroom to a potential "real" audience that students would find easier to visualize. Instead of writing for the teacher, students can write a specialized kind of report for a particular audience. The audience can be more immediate than the usual generalized research audience or even more demanding in that they are in "the real world." For example, a report on a neighborhood survey can be sent with a cover letter to the city council. A suggestion for the improvement of a manufactured product can be sent to the company which produces it. Or students can direct their research efforts toward classmates, as in the suggestion for abstracts described below.

Editing and the Whole Writing Process

Because of the complexity of research tasks, students need to rely on their experience with the writing process while working on research projects. Students need time for pre-writing, incubation periods, first drafts and revisions, and an objective eye for proofreading and editing. Because of the scholarly audience normal for research projects, mechanical accuracy is all the more important; the expectation of accuracy is also particularly hard to fulfill. By assigning research papers due at the end of a term and by asking only for the finished, edited version, teachers miss the chance to help their students with the process of writing. As in all writing, the evaluation of the finished task is not as much help to students as guidance along the way.

Students should be helped at every stage of the writing process, the earlier the better. In selecting topics worthy of research or workable angles on a topic, students can build on questions that have come up in their journal writing or small group discussions. Stimulating films or first-hand experiences can be the take-off points. Even when the teacher knows ahead of time what the research projects will be, activities can be set up to integrate research topics with the rest of the classwork. In short, some attention should be paid to the connection between writers and topics.

Beyond that, teachers could allow time for revising and editing in class. If small groups are regularly used for other purposes, this activity will seem more natural. Not only will students increase each other's awareness of audience needs by asking questions about unclear parts of the papers, but they will also be exchanging content information in these sessions. In that sense revising sessions are substantive and should not be thought of as "time out" from the main business of the course. If students are unused to working together in small groups, then the teacher may have to take on the same function: advising the students about what needs arranging, clarifying, expanding, deleting.

Teachers' comments at the point of revision are much more valuable than they are on the finished copy for the obvious reason that the paper is still in process. However, something is lost by having the teacher serve this revising function. From then on the student is trying to do what the teacher wants rather than what the paper requires. In other words, it is difficult for students to conceive of the teacher as both coach and judge. Figure 5.2 represents a revision worksheet that could be used either by small groups or by the teacher in providing assistance at this crucial time in the writing of a research paper.

If students are quite inexperienced with writing long papers and with revising, it might be well to begin with more focused revising strategies than the comprehensive group activity described in Figure 5.3. Students might be asked first to help each other with some more particular revising strategy. For example, students could help each other add coherence to their papers by adding appropriate transition words from the list in Figure 5.3. A specific revising task sometimes accomplishes an attitude change: that good writing takes repeated manipulation and does not usually emerge full-blown on the first try.

FIGURE 5.2
_____

SAMPLE REVISION WORKSHEET

(To be used in small groups)

DIRECTIONS:
After hearing the writer read his or her own paper, each member of the group completes this sheet and gives it to the writer. You may ask to see the paper if you cannot remember enough by hearing it read. Remember not to focus on spelling or grammar, but on things like organization, audience, purpose, and thesis. Do one person's paper at a time before going on to the next.

Title of the Paper ————————————————————————————

Name of the Writer ———————————————————————————

Name of the Reader ———————————————————————————

1. How would you explain the purpose or main idea of the paper?
   How could this be made more clear?

2. What questions does the paper leave unanswered in your mind? What would you like to hear more about?

FIGURE 5.2 (continued)

SAMPLE REVISION WORKSHEET

3. Who is the intended audience and how can you tell?
   What else might be done to appeal to this or a better audience?

4. What is the organizational plan?
   Suggest some better or additional ways to improve the organization.

5. Use the space below to suggest other revisions you would make in this paper.

FIGURE 5.3

SAMPLE FOCUSED REVISING WORKSHEET: ADDING TRANSITION WORDS

DIRECTIONS:
After dividing into editing groups, have each person read his or her own paper out loud twice. Other group members should keep this list available. On the second time through, interrupt the writer with suggestions of transition words that could be added to clarify the relationship between two sentences or two ideas. Add only a few; don't overdo it.

Meaning	Use			
in addition to	furthermore	also	next	equally important
	moreover	too	first	finally
	besides	like	last	
	likewise	again	lastly	
comparison	similarly			
	likewise			
	in like manner			
contrast	but	nevertheless		
	however	on the other hand		
	still	on the contrary		
	otherwise	although this may be true		
	after all			
result	therefore	consequently		
	hence	as a result		
	accordingly			
time	here	immediately		
	by that time	soon		
	meanwhile	in the meantime		
	at length	afterwards		
	later			
place	here	opposite to		
	by that	across from		
	there	next to		
	beyond	beside		
	nearby			
summary or repetition	to sum up	as I have said	in fact	
	in brief	in other words	for instance	
	on the whole	as has been noted	indeed	
	in short	for example	in any event	

Source: From Sylvia Spann and Mary Beth Culp, Eds., *Thematic Units in Teaching English and the Humanities.* Urbana, Illinois: National Council of Teachers of English, 1975, p. 64.

Both students and teachers often make the same mistake when responding to papers for the purpose of encouraging revision. That is, they call attention to errors in spelling or sentence structure which are rightfully a part of the final writing stage of editing. There is no use correcting individual sentences which will be eliminated or expanded during the revision stage. However, once the revised version is written out, then small groups might again be used for the purpose of editing. The ready availability of a school-wide handbook is helpful for this activity. If and when schools begin to use word processors, then the editing function will become a routine matter. Inexperienced writers tend not to recognize their own errors and they may not be very useful in spotting errors by others. Groups who have worked together, however, come to know which of their members is skillful with editing. Figure 5.4 represents the type of worksheet which might offer these groups the proper focus for editing.

Some teachers feel uncomfortable with using students to find each other's errors on the grounds that students *should* be able to do this for themselves even though teamwork on writing projects is the norm in the publishing and business worlds. Other teachers feel uncomfortable about allowing errors to go by unmarked on early drafts, believing that the mistake is somehow being reinforced by being allowed to repeat itself. As noted in Chapter 2, such a belief presupposes a level of "print-awareness" that may not be characteristic of certain students. (For a fuller discussion of ways to treat errors in early drafts, see Chapter 8.)

The important point is that students should be aware of the differences between revising for content, effectiveness, and organization and editing for surface structure details. Revising occurs midway through the writing process, editing at the end of the writing process.

UNUSUAL RESEARCH ASSIGNMENTS

Given the complexity of research tasks, it is worth simplifying those variables that can be manipulated. Normally teachers assign general topics more or less related to the course material. Often these topics are too general or too broad for easy coverage without special help in selecting a particular slant or emphasis. Yet, teachers specify only some of the traits expected in the finished paper, such as the length. Other parameters of the task—the purpose, the audience, the tone, even the conventions of documentation—are assumed rather than specified. Usually the finished paper is collected and evaluated at the end of the term with neither intervening instruction nor follow-up activities linking it with the other work in the course. As such, the research paper resembles a take-home test more than a well-planned instructional activity.

FIGURE 5.4
_____

SAMPLE EDITING WORKSHEET

(To be used in triads or pairs)

DIRECTIONS:
After reading someone else's paper all the way through, look at it closely for errors in spelling, grammar, sentence structure, and other oversights. Use a pencil and standard proofreading symbols (see handbook) to mark errors on the paper itself. Use this checklist to make sure you have read through the paper carefully enough to evaluate each of these considerations. Give the writer this sheet.

Title of the Paper _____

Name of the Writer _____

Name of the Reader _____

(1 is low, 4 is high)

1. *Spelling*   1   2   3   4
   Note any patterns of misspellings:

2. *Sentence Structure*   1   2   3   4
   Note any error patterns or suggestions for more effective
   sentences:

3. *Grammar*   1   2   3   4
   Note any relevant rules on subject-verb agreement, pro-
   noun reference, pronoun form, etc.:

4. *Paragraph cohesion*   1   2   3   4
   Make suggestions for kinds of transitions or changes in
   order which would improve the paragraphs:

5. *Documentation*   1   2   3   4
   Note any misunderstandings about quoting, marking
   titles, placing footnotes, etc.:

_____

In actuality there are almost limitless variations possible on the research theme. By changing or eliminating some of the more difficult components of research and by encouraging unusual purposes or audiences, the teacher can enhance the students' chances of success. Students can gain confidence in one sub-skill at a time so that more complex assignments are possible later. Unusual assignments, by virtue of their accessibility and novelty, are likely to interest students more, promoting both livelier classes and better attitudes toward writing than would otherwise be the case.

Mentioned below are several research projects which might be termed unusual. Most of them are adaptable to various subjects and ability levels. All of them serve a double pedagogical purpose: they promote writing ability and they teach content.

Interviewing

One way to encourage notetaking as a part of the research project and to separate it from the domination of the copy machine is to use interviews as a source for research papers. Although interviews can be tape recorded (the aural equivalent of the copy machine), that process is often cumbersome, and it can inhibit the free flow of conversation. Besides, the problem of notetaking is not eliminated by a recorder; it is just postponed until the tape is listened to later. Students who take notes during or immediately after an interview are practicing the art of condensation (unless they know shorthand). Recording the main ideas of a dialogue is an excellent way to learn notetaking.

The experience is excellent in other ways as well. The presence of the interviewee lends an immediacy to the information that is more compelling than the appeal of the printed page. Further, students involved in interviewing are caught up in the social role of scholar by virtue of their inquiring stance. Thus the experience is likely to promote a good attitude toward gathering information. The role of interviewer, incidentally, is one that inexperienced writers are quite familiar with because of the frequency of interviews on television. In fact, if the interview is to be reported in dialogue, most students will also be familiar with this format since interviews are popular in newspapers and magazines. Thus the format has a familiar feel and makes a good entrée into research.

In spite of the familiarity of the format, however, most students need considerable guidance in conducting and recording interviews. The hardest problems seem to be asking open-ended questions and building on hints dropped in interviewee's answers rather than moving through a list of questions. Ironically, both of these shortcomings may reflect inadequacies in the way *students* have been questioned by their teachers over the years, always asked the obvious and not drawn out when there has been more to say. Nevertheless, students can be rehearsed into an effective interviewing technique, especially with occasional in-class practice interviewing fellow students as they role-play historic figures. Outside speakers and interviewees may be brought in to supplement class activities. Figure 5.5 lists some guidelines for effective interviewing.

Interviews, with or without supplemental background reading, are viable sources for research in virtually every discipline. Older relatives and neighbors who have lived through earlier eras make excellent resources for political science and history. Professional people and writers are excellent resources for business, social studies, and English. Scientists and doctors are excellent resources for biology, physics, and math. Poets, newspaper writers, and even business people who rely on written communication are usually happy to talk about their craft. Local organizations, such as fine arts groups, the League of Women Voters, or special interest lobbies, often furnish speakers or interviewees for school use.

Every community seems to have plenty of individuals with credentials and willingness to serve as important resources for research projects. And the interviewing process seems particularly promising as an introductory research method, partly because it produces primary materials which require young writers to filter and interpret extensive data, but also because the format is accessible and the personal dimension makes a good transition between private experience and the more distant resources available through printed matter.

Book Reviews and Abstracts

If the ability to summarize is a major goal of a research project, then the assignment could build on in-depth analysis of a single source. Book reviews and abstracts are examples of this type of assignment. The book review, when it goes beyond mere summary to an evaluation of the book's strengths and weaknesses, is by far the more traditional assignment. The abstract is a specialized version of a book review, focusing as it does on a particular reader's needs (usually scholars who need guidance in deciding whether they should read the longer piece that the abstract is based on). Certain difficulties present themselves to writers of either the book review or the abstract: how to refer to the author (by his or her last name) and how to use quotations. Again, the availability of model papers is the best way to call attention to these techniques.

The abstract is a preview summary of a longer work. To write an abstract students must be able to interpret the longer piece of writing, identify the thesis, and select relevant subpoints without distorting the emphasis of the original. Since abstracts are usually written to introduce potential readers to a longer piece, students need to recognize their readers' needs as they write an abstract. Some abstracts are more than descriptive; they criticize or evaluate the original.

Abstracts, like book reviews, are usually written in complete sentences using subordinate clauses to cut down on wordage. Ab-

FIGURE 5.5

INTERVIEW GUIDELINES

1. Plan the questions you will ask and put them on a tablet you can write on during the interview, leaving enough space between questions to jot down answers.

2. In planning the questions, be conscious of two considerations:
   a. Start with the most general questions (asking for background information, description of experiences, or other questions which might be answered with a story).
   b. Phrase questions in such a way that they can't be answered with "yes," "no," or single words—ask how and why questions.

3. Try to ask the questions in an order that each new question will build on the previous one, e.g., from background to specific details, from principles to applications, etc.

4. Show that you are a good listener by doing the following:
   a. Instead of moving on to the next question after each answer, try to reword what the person just said and ask if you got it right.
   b. Ask for definitions, especially of words that are simple, but could mean many things, like "happy," "interesting," "dangerous," etc.
   c. Pick up on dropped hints of something the interviewee may want to talk more about—even though you had not planned to ask about that.
   d. Bring the interviewee back on task if he or she talks too much about irrelevant things.
   e. If ideas are left too general, ask for examples. If there are too many details, ask for the principles or main ideas that tie things together.

5. Come to the interview prepared: know your interviewee's name, title, company or affiliation, and something of the topic under consideration.

6. Take simple notes throughout, but copy whole phrases when you think the interviewee has said something you'd like to quote. Ask for spellings and repetitions of key facts if necessary, but try to keep the conversation flowing. The interviewee should never have to wait while you write.

7. Be courteous. Begin and end the session with polite, friendly conversation of a general nature. Ask permission if you intend to tape record. Speak loudly enough. Write a follow-up thank-you note.

stracts eliminate introductions and details while preserving the organizational scheme of the original. The length varies from one paragraph to several. Thus abstracts are really just summaries with a definite purpose and a specified audience.

Sometimes students write abstracts of their research sources and these are duplicated for distribution to the whole class. Figure 5.6 represents such an assignment.

Students in an anthropology class found and previewed one source of potential use to their classmates. Thus the assignment minimized the work involved in locating resources. Yet each student had access to a wide range of information for later projects, a debate, and a persuasive paper. In this assignment, students distributed their abstracts to the class as a preliminary to taking orders for copies of notes or photocopied pages. One further advantage to the assignment, a finished sample of which is included in Figure 5.7, is that it provided students with a sense of audience and purpose.

Problem-solving and Lab Reports

Aware that taking a special slant on a topic is an integral part of the

---

FIGURE 5.6

SAMPLE ABSTRACT ASSIGNMENT

Anthropology 101
Fall Semester
Ms. Cholak, Instructor

Due: October 1

As part of our study of American Indian culture, we will later hold a class debate on a controversial legal case involving Indian fishing rights. In preparation for that debate you will all collect information about the American Indian situation. If each person finds one good source and shares it, we will each have less work to do in the library. Therefore, we will each do that, writing a one-page abstract of what we find for distribution in class.

An abstract is a brief summary of a longer piece of writing. Its purpose is to inform the reader of the kinds of information contained in the longer piece so that the reader can decide whether to read the longer piece or not.

The abstract should begin with a full bibliographic entry (so that the reader can find the book or article later). Normally, of course, bibliographic entries appear in the bibliography at the end of a research paper, but ours will appear right across the top of the page. That way it will be highly visible and will make the abstract a kind of annotation of the bibliographic entry.

The abstract should contain a summary of the content of the longer piece. It should be written in your own words except for those phrases or sentences quoted. Furthermore, the abstract should give the reader some idea of the length of the longer piece, the kinds of illustrations it has, the level of difficulty, and other information which may be pertinent to our debate.

Finally, our abstracts for this class should be written on ditto. We will explain what we have found to the whole class and take orders for one of the following:

1. photocopies of the original
2. clear notes on the original

Be sure to state which option you're offering and give the class a price range per page.

On the day we share abstracts every class member will take orders for copies of what he or she has found. People placing orders will have to pay. Using this system, we will each have access to all the information without each having to spend too much time hunting up sources.

A sample abstract is attached.

---

organizing process, some teachers choose to limit research topics in such a way as to suggest a method of organization, thus relieving students of that consideration in completing their research project. One way to do this is to set up the task to resemble a lab report where direct observation replaces consultation of written texts to a certain extent, with perhaps some background reading preliminary to an experiment. Another way is to set up the task in a problem-solving format whereby alternative solutions are listed and discussed as a means of justifying the best solution, which is advocated in the conclusion.

Most science texts prescribe a set format for the lab report with lists of materials, procedures, and results. Prefacing one of these with a summary of relevant information from the textbook or other outside source makes for an excellent introduction to research techniques in science. Chapters 2 and 4 also suggest some ways that records be kept on such experiments with running commentaries on the problems and questions raised along the way. These records then serve as source material for the final paper in much the same way as other reference material. They are data to be summarized and condensed by the writer.

Redi's classic experiment to disprove the spontaneous generation of maggots in meat is an excellent example of the kind of experiment conducive to this type of research report.[2] Meat is placed in three jars, one uncovered, one covered with cheesecloth, and one covered with clear plastic or glass. Flies are attracted to the two jars with meat they can smell, but they will only infest the open jar. Students using this experiment as the core of their research paper would use their records of observation as primary data and interpret and organize the information from that source just as they would from a printed source in a more traditional assignment.

In a problem-solving project the writer is also encouraged to follow a specific format, usually an extended summary of the known factors in the problem itself followed by a listing of the pro's and con's for each potential solution. Often students are motivated to consult outside sources of similar cases or additional data. The problem should elicit information already covered in the classwork or text, but also go beyond this toward original assimilation of new materials. In a geography class students could be shown a map of Central America. Then they could be asked to recommend and justify an alternate canal route in Nicaragua, Panama, or Colombia.[3] To do this they would need access to census data, information about the terrain, and economic statistics. A favorite of history and political science teachers is to change the outcome of some battle or political event and then allow students to hypothesize the course of events that might result. Students must justify their choice on the basis of facts, trends, and analogous situations known to them or available in directed reading.

Such problem-solving assignments are effective because the

FIGURE 5.7

SAMPLE ABSTRACT

Astrov, Margot, Ed. American Indian Prose and Poetry. New York: Capricorn
    Books, 1962.

This 366-page paperback contains several kinds of information
useful for the Indian debate. First of all, there is a lengthy introduction
by the editor with information about Indian beliefs regarding the
special function of words and the effects of white missionaries
on Indian culture. The main part of the book contains sample Indian
myths and poems, often completely explained through lengthy
footnotes. Finally, there is an extensive bibliography of other books
and articles on Indian literature and beliefs. An index is helpful for
locating famous people, works from the different tribes, and important
themes.
    Some useful kinds of information concern those myths and
legends which closely parallel Christian Biblical stories. There are also
various stories about how the missionaries could have done a better
job of trying to fit in with Indian beliefs. The Indians apparently have
a higher regard for language than we do. They consider that even
though they stay behind, the women who chant are doing just as much
work as the hunters. Another interesting phenomenon concerns
private visions recalled in poetry. Indian braves depend on these secret
words to give them power in times of hardship. Still another function
of language concerns the use of words by medicine men for curing
sickness. This book also contains newspaper coverage of utterances by
famous Indians such as Sitting Bull. It becomes evident that Americans
didn't understand the Indian's way of using metaphors to come at
meaning indirectly. You come away from this book somewhat
discouraged about all those broken treaties and with a different view
of the so-called Indian uprisings.

organization of the final paper is prescribed, and yet the student writer is experiencing a sense of creativity in what he selects and writes, a freedom all too often lacking in traditional research assignments. Of course the particularity of the focus also eliminates some of the possibilities for plagiarism.

Case Studies

In the social sciences a problem-solving task often takes the form of a case study. A case is a particular instance, a real person or situation, that illustrates some general principles or clarifies some theory. Although case studies can focus on past events or historical figures, their special features show to better advantage when the subject involves observation of a case in process. Good subjects include structured observations of small children to illustrate developmental stages in psychology, structured observation of legislative bodies passing laws to illustrate governmental action, or structured observation of school events to illustrate sociological theories.

Each of these tasks encourages disciplined observation, interpretation of these observations according to abstract principles, categorization of data, and analysis of implications. Additionally, the written reports must be characterized by an objective tone, a requirement which in and of itself presents problems to an inexperienced writer more used to reading the subjective accounts characteristic of fiction. (This, incidentally, illustrates once again the necessity of having model papers available to familiarize students with the kind of accomplishment they are supposed to achieve.) Especially when some sort of recommendation or conclusion is to be drawn from the study will students need guidance and supervision along the way. Careful record-keeping and speculative writing must, therefore, be a requirement if case studies are to be assigned.

Ideally students would alternate observation periods with small group discussions among classmates working on similar projects. The exchange of information and oral rehearsal of explanations serve several crucial purposes: students can help each other distinguish between value-laden reports and objective accounts; they can help each other analyze data according to relevant interpretive principles; and they can compare and contrast information, clearing up misconceptions in the process.

The advantages of case studies over traditional research papers are many. First of all, the details come from first-hand observation rather than secondary sources. As has already been mentioned, inexperienced writers are more likely to become personally involved with materials they actually experience rather than distillations of first-hand experiences recorded in other people's writing. In addition to the immediacy of the first-hand experience, case studies also promote notetaking and expressive writing since each student must generate his or her own data. Yet the usual problems of citation and documentation are not an issue (unless the case study includes reference to written sources as well as direct observation). The narrative organizational plan, controlled by the chronological unfolding of events, is relatively easy for inexperienced writers to present. And, finally, case studies encourage a natural kind of analysis as course concepts must guide and control the selective observation of relatively complex data.

Debates and Persuasive Papers

The assignment described above involving the kind of book review known as an *abstract* is merely the first step of a series of class events building on research done by class members. The abstract is preparation for a debate which then leads to a set of persuasive papers. Ultimately, each student is expected to write an argumentative essay in support of one side of a controversial issue. It is easy to imagine such issues in social studies classes, but literature classes sometimes lend themselves to controversial issues as well: whether a given character was treated fairly, whether a character made the best choice(s), and so forth. Essays developing a personal opinion and substantiating that opinion by reference to outside sources represent one end of a continuum of possible research projects. Here the students are subordinating research findings—using them often quite sparingly—to their own ideas. At the opposite end of that research continuum are the kinds of reports more traditionally associated with research papers, reports which merely summarize what other people have written. Persuasive papers, because they involve a high degree of analytic ability, are best reserved for students in late adolescence and beyond. Even then some form of pre-writing or warm-up should precede the actual writing of the essays if superficiality and overgeneralizations are to be avoided.

    A good way to prepare students for persuasive research papers is to stage class debates. Students love the drama of a debate and usually enjoy the purposefulness of doing research in preparation for one. Preparing for a debate is also a good way to spur lots of expressive writing and small group discussion, both of which activate passive students. Such preparation might be considered pre-writing (for the persuasive paper) at its very best.

    Establishing the ground rules for a debate will vary from class to class, but the following factors have to be considered:

1. The topic must be controversial enough to have a pro- side and a

con- side. The topic also must be legitimate enough to engage students voluntarily, but not so controversial as to alarm their parents. Good topics are those currently in the news: capital punishment, but not homosexuality; the Equal Rights Amendment, but not theories of creation or evolution.

2. Arguments should be supported by researched data, not merely opinions or personal experiences.
3. Students should be allowed to argue (at least initially) on the side of their choice so that they have a genuine stake in the outcome and do not participate in a detached or silly way.
4. Individuals and teams should be allowed adequate time to plan and to rehearse arguments. They must also consider arguments the other side will be advancing so that they will be able to rebut those arguments.
5. Some provision should be made for seeing or hearing a real debate before staging one. This provision is similar to the necessity of viewing model papers before writing one. School debate teams or videotapes of professional teams are ideal for this purpose.
6. In more advanced courses preparation can include the study of logical fallacies. Logical fallacies should be avoided, but might be used deliberately by one team if the other team is not alert enough in pointing them out. Figure 5.8 is a list of logical fallacies which should be understood and illustrated prior to a debate or the writing of persuasive papers.
7. Simplified rules can be outlined ahead of time, preferably with score-keeping done by fellow students as a means of involving the whole class in the debate process.

Generally class debates are most successful when they involve debate teams of five to seven members. That way each team member has an important part to play, and no one can rely on the class leaders to carry the whole load. The class divides into teams, but not necessarily evenly (if students are allowed to choose the side they are to represent). Ideally there will be as many pro- teams as con- teams so that separate debates can be scheduled for each pairing. When someone is absent or the teams are not evenly matched numerically, some students will have to do more work. When fewer teams represent one side or the other, they may have to debate more often, representing their viewpoint in several contests. In other words, the same issue can be argued multiple times in the same class, and both sides will improve and expand their arguments if adequate follow-up discussion is included as one part of the debate program.

By appointing a student to be the timekeeper, the teacher will be free to keep a score sheet and to jot down notes for the follow-up discussion. First one team presents its arguments and then the other team attempts to rebut those arguments. Next, the other team presents its arguments and is, in turn, rebutted. At the end each team makes a concluding statement.

Each team member is allowed up to two minutes to advance one aspect of the team's argument—the general principle, an explanation, and its support. After each team member has made an opening statement, the opposing team members take turns pointing out the weaknesses in the opening statements (but not advancing their own arguments, since that would pre-empt their own presentation). This rebuttal period can last from five to eight minutes, depending on the time period allotted for the debate. No student should make a second rebuttal until each other student on that team has made at least one rebuttal. Members of the first team may not answer this rebuttal at all, but they may jot down what they would like to answer and pass these notes along to the team member they have selected for the two-minute closing statement. Now the second team makes its opening statements, each member taking up to two minutes to announce, explain, and support one aspect of their argument. The members of the first team take

---

FIGURE 5.8
_____

LOGICAL FALLACIES

1. *Ad hominem*—"to the man";—insulting the speaker

    usually means insulting the person's character, but can also be used for accepting something as true *because* of the person advocating it

    e.g. Anyone who is against capital punishment must be crazy.

2. *Red herring*—fish used to block the scent of a hunted animal—irrelevant argument

    e.g. I may not know much about capital punishment, but I saw a man drown once.

3. *Hasty generalization*—drawing a conclusion from one or two examples

    sub-type: *stereotype*—a generalization about groups whereby all members are presumed to be the same

    e.g. Both men I saw on death row were white; therefore, I would conclude that most killers are white.

4. *False analogy*—comparison between two unlike things that works in some ways, but not in all ways.

    e.g. Capital punishment is the same as natural selection: it's just a way of weeding out the less desirable members of the species.

5. *Faulty cause*—assuming that one thing caused another just because it occurred first

    e.g. I know that man was guilty because three days earlier I saw him at the scene of the crime.

FIGURE 5.8 (continued)

LOGICAL FALLACIES

6. *Either/or*—taking a complex issue and making it seem that there are only two ways of looking at it

> e.g. Either you think that handguns cause murders or else you think that their availability has no effect on murders committed.

7. *Appeal to history*—assuming that something is right just because it's been done that way a long time or used to be done that way

> e.g. Capital punishment must be right because some form of it has been used in every culture.

8. *Everyone is doing it*—assuming something is right just because it is widespread

> e.g. Television shows could not influence crimes because everybody watches television.

9. *Appeal to emotions*—making you feel bad or good about something and so avoiding the logic of the issue

> e.g. Capital punishment is as American as motherhood and apple pie.

10. *Guilt (or praise) by association*—assuming something is right or wrong because something or someone associated with it is right or wrong

> e.g. Any friend of Caryl Chessman deserves to be shot.

---

turns pointing out weaknesses in the second team's argument for five to eight minutes. Once again the rebuttal may not be answered except later through the one person selected to make the second team's closing statement. These "rules" are summarized in Figure 5.9.

The debate must be started promptly and carefully timed so that it can be completed within a thirty-five minute or fifty-minute time period. At the end observers will also need at least five minutes to tally their scores before any discussion ensues. A debate simply cannot be interrupted and begun again on another day.

A simple way to score is to have each observer keep a record of points awarded for each good reason, good explanation, good support offered, or effective rebuttal comment. Figure 5.10 presents a sample score sheet using this system.

Although individuals will differ in their awarding of points, winners can be determined simply by totaling the points awarded by all observers. Generally a grade is superfluous. The honor of winning is enough credit for motivation, yet losers will not feel so bad if they have not received thereby a lower grade. There is anxiety already over the necessity of speaking out and the novelty of depending on teamwork, so the pressure of being graded is counter-productive. At any

FIGURE 5.9

RULES FOR A DEBATE

1. Flip a coin to decide which team starts. That team will be Team A.
2. *Opening statements—Team A:* Each member presents one aspect of their side of the argument, including some explanation and support. Support can take the form of statistics, cases, quotations by authorities, etc. There is a two-minute time limit for each team member, but the full two minutes need not be used. While Team A is presenting these opening statements, Team B should be taking notes for the rebuttal.
3. *Rebuttal—Team B:* Members take turns pointing out weaknesses in the opening statements made by Team A, including any logical fallacies noted. No students should make a second rebuttal until each other student on Team B has made at least one. There is a total time limit of five to eight minutes rather than a limit on each rebuttal. Members of Team A may not answer, but should take notes to pass to their team member selected for the closing statement.
4. *Opening statements—Team B* (as per Rule 2).
5. *Rebuttal—Team B* (as per Rule 3).
6. *Closing statement—Team A:* One member summarizes the best of Team A's arguments and puts to rest any claims made during the rebuttal of Team A's opening statements.
7. *Closing statement—Team B:* (Same as Rule 6).

Note:
Each team should come prepared with notes in readily accessible form, having already planned who will say what.

---

rate, students know that their persuasive papers, inspired by the debate, will indeed be graded.

Actually the follow-up writing and discussion are more important for the persuasive paper than the debate itself. The follow-up activities allow for reflection and speculation so that the persuasive paper will not represent the first and most obvious arguments that come to mind. While the observers are tallying their scores, the debaters themselves should jot down their preliminary reactions to what they have just experienced, what worked and what didn't work and why. If possible, the observers, too, should be allowed to write expressively before the debate is discussed. The score sheets and the written reactions will serve as records of the event and will bring out more insights than would occur otherwise. A tape recording or videotape of the debate would be even more valuable as a record and could be analyzed later by the whole class or some members of it. After the follow-up discussion students should be asked to summarize what they learned and express any new ideas that have come to them.

The combination of research, debate, and persuasive paper is ideal as a writing assignment for many reasons: it combines purposefulness, sense of a real audience, values clarification, good listening, lots of chances for talk, and personal involvement in what amounts

FIGURE 5.10

_____

SAMPLE DEBATE SCORE SHEET

Directions:
Single points can be awarded for:

1. Opening statements that are clearly explained and adequately supported.
2. Use of a logical fallacy that the other team doesn't catch in the rebuttal.
   (You can mark a point, then erase it later if the other team catches it.)
3. Evidence that a team member changed what he or she meant to say because of what another member had already said.
4. Correct identification of a logical fallacy in the other team's statement.
5. Good rebuttal—can be pointing out poor explanation, faulty support, or a good question about something left unsaid.

TEAM A MEMBERS	OPENING STATEMENT	REBUTTAL	CLOSING
TEAM B MEMBERS			

_____

to a rehearsal for an advanced writing task. There are many other activities which call forth some of these virtues—panel discussions, skits, and the preparation of documentaries, for example—but none seem to have the competitive edge that debates have for sparking introspective thinking and causing students to use writing as a tool rather than self-consciously as an end-in-itself.

GOOD DIRECTIONS

Although instructors should be aware of all the factors described above, it would be overwhelming for students to be told everything as part of their directions for a research paper task. Indeed, the rule should be simplicity when it comes to directions. If model papers are provided and discussed for what they reveal about appropriate topics, tone, and format, then specific directions should be written so that they can be referred to at crucial times, such as during the writing process itself. The directions should include the following:

1. Restrictions on topic
2. Expected length
3. Deadlines (better if done with checkpoints)
4. Restrictions (with a note to refer to sample papers) as to margins, pagination, citation method, and examples of bibliographical entries
5. Some acknowledgement of the processes involved
6. Reference to purpose and audience (the reason for all the rules on documentation)
7. Indication of how the writing will be evaluated (especially if rough drafts and notecards are to be turned in)

In many ways these suggestions parallel the guidelines offered in Chapter 2 as good directions for assignments. Figure 5.11 is an example of good directions for a research paper.

EVALUATION

Finally, the teacher is faced with the task of grading the research paper. Here again there are many options. Ideally the specific criteria have been clearly stated as part of the directions given for the assignment. If attention has been given to revision and editing prior to the submission of the final paper, then the teacher need not make extensive corrections or comments. Generally the most effective way of grading research projects is via a checklist similar to the one pictured in Figure 5.12, but adapted to the particular assignment at hand. This should be combined with some comment on the content of the paper, stated politely and appreciatively. There should be some reference in these comments as to why the handling of the content resulted in the particular grade assigned. When comments are limited to matters of form or documentation, rather than being context-specific, they seem to lay an exaggerated importance on these features. In actuality, surface structure errors usually co-occur with the more serious conceptual oversights which are the rightful domain of the content teacher.

FIGURE 5.11

SAMPLE DIRECTIONS FOR A RESEARCH PROJECT

Biology 150
Spring Semester, 1982
R. Kaufman, Instructor

DROSOPHILA PROBLEM/SOLUTION PAPER ——→ *restriction on topic*

DIRECTIONS:
Follow the procedures for using Drosophila to
prove Mendel's genetic theories as outlined in   *acknowledgment*
The Carolina Drosophila Manual. Keep careful   *of processes*
records of the equipment and timing of your   *involved*
anesthetizing, separating, and counting of the
fruit flies. Then write a formal paper in which
you summarize the theory and your expectations
for verifying it. Organize your paper around the   *purpose and*
problems you encountered, concluding with   *audience*
suggestions for next term's students, who might
be asked to complete this same experiment. Con-   *manuscript*
sult the folder on reserve in the library for sample *restrictions*
papers from past classes done in the format appropriate for scientific reports.

LENGTH:
Approximately four typed pages   ——→ *expected length*

BIBLIOGRAPHY:
Your textbook
The Carolina Drosophila Manual
At least one other article from among those on
reserve

EVALUATION:
Journal records on time . . . 10 pts.
First draft on time . . . . 10 pts.
Revised draft on time . . . . . 10 pts.
(3 points off for each day late on each part of   *evaluation*
the task)   *criteria*

Typed manuscript on time . . . 70 pts.
   clear theory & plan (20 pts.)
   organization, main body (20 pts.)
   effective conclusion (10 pts.)
   mechanics (10 pts.)
   manuscript form (10 pts.)

DEADLINES:
Experiment completed, journal in 3/30   *early*
Rough draft for in-class revision 4/4   *checkpoints*
Revised draft for editing 4/10   *and deadlines*
Finished manuscript 4/13

FIGURE 5.12
_____

SAMPLE CHECKLIST FOR THE DROSOPHILA PROBLEM/
SOLUTION PAPER (Figure 5.11)

				Points awarded
EARLY SUBMISSIONS:				
Journal record of experiment (out of 10)				_____
First draft (out of 10)				_____
Revised draft (out of 10)				_____
FINISHED MANUSCRIPT: Clarity of theory	poor	average	good	
Clarity of plan				
Way sources used				
Introduction Total (Out of 20)				_____
Identification of problems	poor	average	good	
Alternation of generalizations and details				
Main Body Total (Out of 20)				_____
Insightful conclusion	poor	average	good	
Related to body				
Conclusion Total (Out of 10)				_____
Spelling	poor	average	good	
Punctuation				
Sentence structure				
Mechanics Total (Out of 10)				_____
Bibliography	poor	average	good	
Level of formality				
Format Total (Out of 10)				_____

GRAND TOTAL (OUT OF 100) _____

FIGURE 5.12 (continued)

SAMPLE CHECKLIST FOR THE DROSOPHILA PROBLEM/
SOLUTION PAPER (Figure 5.11)

CONTEXT-SPECIFIC COMMENTS:

Your grade of B reflects the good work you did in recording the experiment in your journal. If you were to go back to those records later you might have data for future genetic experiments. If you were to improve the present experiment, however, you'd need better insights about what went wrong. It is not enough to suggest that "things went wrong" – you needed to explain the problem of fruit flies hatching at night and mating before they could be separated. Next term's students would need more warning about specific things they should be careful about. The lapses into slang are humorous for our purposes, but would be inappropriate in a lab setting. Overall your attention to detail, even with the proofreading, reveals your consideration for potential readers of your report.

INTERPRETATION OF POINTS:
90–100 = A; 80–89 = B; 70–79 = C; 60–69 = D

Some people like to encourage attention to detail by offering to raise grades for papers that are revised or edited after they have been turned in for evaluation. Such an option may in fact encourage sloppiness initially, certainly it misplaces the purpose of revision, which is not for a higher grade but for a more effective piece of communication. Perhaps a better means of forcing attention to overlooked details is to grade the piece and offer it back for correction with the threat of a lowered grade if it is not corrected within a certain period of time.[4] Chapter 8 includes some additional suggestions for ways to evaluate student writing.

One further comment on grading: in no course should the writing done be limited to what receives a grade. The research project, taking as much time and effort as it does, should definitely be graded rather than merely "counted for credit." On the other hand, various earlier tasks, such as turning in note cards or early drafts, can be "counted for credit" or assigned points contributing to the total grade. In any case, other ungraded writing tasks must be part of the coursework if a change in attitude toward writing is one of the course goals. Writing must be rewarded when it is well done, but it must be encouraged and experienced as a worthwhile activity for itself in noncompetitive contexts as well.

PLAGIARISM

A delicate issue at grading time concerns what to do about plagiarism, the deliberate copying of someone else's work with the intention of passing it off as one's own. It used to be that students were expelled or failed for proven plagiarism, but the plagiarism issue is no longer clear-cut. Also, plagiarism is not always clearly recognizable. Intentional plagiarism is sometimes hard to distinguish from mistakes attributable to inexperience. As has already been suggested, however, plagiarism becomes nearly impossible when attention is regularly given to the process of composing and to individualizing assignments.

FIGURE 5.13
_____
SAMPLE STATEMENT ON PLAGIARISM*

Plagiarism is the deliberate copying of another person's sentences or ideas without giving him or her due credit. Copied sentences or portions of sentences must always be properly introduced and set off by quotation marks or with special indenting. Your handbook has directions for how this is done.

The way to avoid plagiarism is to take good notes, carefully quoted or in your own words. Do not write directly from photo copies or open books—unless you are quoting them.

You will be suspected of plagiarism whenever what you write closely resembles another piece of writing familiar to your reader, whenever the ideas and sentence structure differ markedly from other things you have written, or whenever you cannot produce notes or early drafts of an obviously revised piece of writing.

Suspected plagiarism in this course will result in your being asked to do the assignment again. Proven plagiarism will result in failure on that assignment.

This policy is not meant to express mistrust of you any more than our government's laws against stealing are meant to express mistrust of the average citizen. Plagiarism is, after all, the academic equivalent of robbery—and innocence is not often accepted as an excuse in either case.

*To be distributed to students prior to giving a research assignment.

Good instruction also prevents plagiarism by attending to the development of skills that make it unnecessary. If plagiarism by oversight or innocence is eliminated, then only deliberate plagiarism will have to be dealt with.

The issue of plagiarism should be discussed before any cases occur. If there is no school-wide policy, then individual teachers should publish their own statement similar to the one in Figure 5.13 with a clear definition, a reason, and a punishment. Generally it is too time-consuming to track down sources and prove plagiarism, so the easiest solution is simply to declare suspected plagiarism as unacceptable for the assignment given. This, of course, is no problem when notecards and rough drafts have been collected earlier and the paper was seen in progress.

Obviously many teachers ignore the plagiarism issue, pointing out the need to assume trust in other school transactions and hating to get into the policeman's role. But looking the other way abdicates responsibility and sets back further the cause of writing and learning. It keeps students from their potential as productive writers and thinkers.

PREPARING STUDENTS FOR WRITING IN A PARTICULAR DISCIPLINE

Ultimately the kinds of writing assigned should prepare students for the kinds of writing typical of a given discipline. Students in particular subjects should learn to observe, think, and communicate in the modes peculiar to that discipline. In this regard no one is better prepared to teach students to write in the tradition of a given discipline than the teacher who has been trained in it. However, teachers must distinguish between the *ultimate* goal and those steps along the way needed to prepare students for that end. Students must not be pushed to write in the tradition of a discipline at younger ages or earlier stages than is really possible.

The research paper is ideally suited to the goal of preparing students for the communication of a particular discipline. The library work can serve as background information as students design and conduct their own original research. Much has been written about science papers in this regard.[5] Advocates of an inductive, experiential approach to science have long recommended the use of writing to encourage hypothesis formation and subsequent experimentation. Similarly, students of sociology should make use of questionnaires and interviews, the standard research tools in their discipline. Psychology and business students should become familiar with the case study. Students of literature will only become confident in interpretation if they respond personally and deeply rather than merely report what scholars have written.

THE VALUE OF RESEARCH PROJECTS

In a sense the research paper, when done correctly, is the apex of achievement in academic writing. It brings together virtually every writing skill which might be practiced in a more limited context. Yet there can be very little carry-over between writing a research paper in one content area and writing papers in another area because of differences in the kinds of material that must be located and the kinds of integrating expected once the information is absorbed. Ironically many teachers assign research papers as their only writing task, due at the end of the course, thereby escaping familiarity with the students' writing problems and avoiding instructional activities which might prepare students for the research project. When students do not or cannot rise to this challenge, teachers sometimes feel justified in dropping this last vestige of practice in writing, thus compounding the literacy problem further.

A more thoughtful approach, following assessment of student performance in writing, would be to offer the research project as part of a series of reading and writing activities carefully designed so that some are ungraded or exploratory while others are more scholarly and refined.

A modified research project, worked on with good attention to the writing processes involved, will do more to promote interest in the subject than any number of lectures or films can. Awareness of options is the key to an experience with research that will result in long-range involvement and satisfaction unheard of where a grade is the only measure of achievement. After all, it is not a mere historical quirk that research papers became the quintessential scholarly task.

NOTES

1. James Moffett, *A Student-Centered Language Arts Program, K–13* (Boston: Houghton Mifflin Co., 1968), 369–370.
2. The experiment is described in detail in Evelyn Morholt, Paul F. Brandwein, and Alexander Joseph, *A Sourcebook for the Biological Sciences*, 2nd ed. (New York: Harcourt, Brace and World, Inc., 1966).
3. This problem is pictured and explained in G.M. Prince, *The Practice of Creativity* (New York: Harper and Row, 1970).
4. Idea from Anne J. Herrington, "Writing to Learn, Writing Across the Disciplines," *College English* 43 (April 1981): 379–387.
5. See, for example, Paul De Hart Hurd, *New Directions in Teaching Secondary School Science* (Chicago: Rand McNally, 1971).

6

Essay Tests

In theory essay tests are a good thing. Students have a chance to practice their writing skills, and they get the message that writing is important to all their teachers. More to the point, students gain practice in selecting relevant facts, combining them in new ways, and integrating information. In short, in writing essays students are operating on a high plane of intellectuality: retrieving discrete bits of information and giving them meaning rather than merely recognizing and manipulating what is given, as is the case with objective tests.

Essays offer more than practice in recalling and organizing data. The essay writer is playing a role quite different from the objective test-taker's role, where the student is understood to be passive and dependent like a defendant at a trial. The teacher-as-prosecutor dominates objective tests, trying, in a sense, to trick the defendant (the test-taker). Thus the student has very little sense of control and very little ownership of the answers, which are counted as "correct" or "incorrect" no matter how ambiguous the question may have been. On the other hand, essay writers play the role of scholar, taking the challenge of the question and answering it with the information they know. Their job is to dazzle, and to do this they need a writer's sense of purpose and good intuitions about their audience (the teacher). Essay test writing can, therefore, be explained as a socializing experience.

PROBLEMS WITH ESSAY TESTS

Essay tests, however, are one more thing that good teachers often give up for the wrong reasons. Some teachers get discouraged because their students are unable to express themselves in writing. Spelling, punctuation, and other errors mar the answers beyond any redeeming advantage. Hence there is worry about giving students a grade in

"English" rather than measuring what they know about the subject at hand. Furthermore, essays by definition can't measure the full range of discrete bits of information "covered" in a course; thus they seem an inefficient method of evaluating what students have learned. Others worry about the time involved in grading essays. And, finally, some teachers acquiesce to their students' antipathy for essay exams, remembering perhaps their own dislike for taking them in times gone by.

Each of these reasons is well founded and deserving of discussion. If students are ill equipped to write essay exams, then it seems likely that they will only be able to learn the material superficially. Yet they cannot improve in writing without practice. Much harm is done to the cause of essay testing when teachers lament what students *should* be able to do rather than recognizing and building on what they *can* do.

As to mechanical errors, this problem, as already mentioned when discussing assessment, is only exacerbated by avoidance. Obviously mechanical errors do affect the quality of an essay and, therefore, can't ever be ignored in evaluating essay answers. In actuality, the presence of gross errors almost always co-occurs with inadequate factual data and organizational skills. Although teachers need not mark errors, these will certainly be factors in assessing the answers. Students should never be told that spelling and sentence structure don't matter. What is true is that the content teacher need not be concerned with teaching or even marking these technical matters. There are various other ways of requiring attention to error-correction without unduly penalizing students who have not mastered these conventions. This will be discussed further later in the chapter.

As to not being able to test all the students know, Americans seem to be obsessed with quantity, and the test-makers' need to measure everything that has been taught is one indication of this. Some teachers have even been known to espouse the theory that students in introductory courses should not write anything: they should wait to integrate until they have learned all the baseline data. Of course, this view of learning, as purely quantitative, pouring information from the teacher's full vessel into the student's empty vessel, is open to debate.

A theme of this book is that writing is a productive process rather than a purely receptive one; it encourages involvement with new information. As such, writing should accompany all stages of the learning process and not just the final ones. Once this point of view is adopted, we will not have the alienation from the writing process that is so typical when writing, on the one hand, is respected so highly that we don't allow students to do it until they have been "initiated," and, on the other hand, so denigrated that it is viewed as inadequate to reveal all a student knows about content.

To solve the problem of "getting at" all that a student knows at test time, two solutions come to mind. First, one could assume the essay answers are merely representative of what the student *also* knows about details not covered. Secondly, one could give a separate objective test in conjunction with the essay test. In either case, it is not advisable to ask such broad questions or so many questions that everything will be covered. That would merely defeat the thoughtful process that essay test-writing is meant to encourage.

Of course, it is the teacher's obligation to recognize the importance of the differences in modes of testing. Essay tests measure a student's comprehension and interpretation of information, the significant relationships inherent in the data. Essay writers in that sense *make* meaning; they *use* their knowledge. Teachers should avoid using essay tests which merely disguise objective questions, that is, questions which ask students to define, list, name, or do other lower-order tasks to determine whether memorizing has been done. There is nothing innately wrong with memorizing, but teachers should ask questions which encourage students to use information rather than merely recall it. Suggestions for implementing this advice appear later in the chapter.

It is true, however, that grading essays is time-consuming in comparison with grading objective tests. Even so, there are shortcuts, especially if the tests are well designed. But teachers must be convinced that the advantages of essays warrant the extra time they take.

WHAT ESSAY TESTS DO TO THE WRITING PROCESS

Some teachers object to essay tests as writing practice because of the artificiality of the time limits imposed. Students have inadequate time to think and no chance to revise. Since there is so little chance to edit, the writing process seems short-circuited. An anxious student may lack the necessary ability to concentrate under such circumstances.

Actually the compression of the planning, revising, and editing stages of composing can be one of the most challenging aspects of essay testing. Well prepared students have brain-stormed potential questions and rehearsed the facts they would muster to answer them. The necessity of writing quickly and in an organized way can be a pleasure in contrast to the writer's block and procrastination which often characterize out-of-class writing. This can be especially true if the test-taker is prepared psychologically, is alert, with adrenalin flowing. The relatively fast flow of words may generate new ideas during the test situation, and when this occurs, learning occurs. The result: Test-Takers' High!

Given the damage that time constraints can do to test perform-ance, however, teachers should make the test experience more amen-able to what we know about the writing process: that writers need a sense of purpose and audience as well as information to convey; that an extended time frame is needed if rumination or proof-reading are to be encouraged; that writers gain a sense of control when they are aware of options; that students learn better the rules of a writing task from reading examples of what is expected than from direct instruc-tion.

Since these considerations are factors in assigning other types of writing, they could be incorporated into the test situation as well. Sample essay answers from earlier tests can be made available for stu-dents to read. Essay questions can even be announced ahead of time (to allow for rumination). Answers can be revised after an initial grad-ing if the educational advantages warrant this. Whenever possible, students should be allowed some choice of topic or approach to the topic.

PROBLEMS FROM THE STUDENTS' POINT OF VIEW

In addition to the time constraints and intellectual demands that sometimes overwhelm students, there are several other kinds of mis-understandings that inhibit performance on essay tests. Students often assume things about essay tests that keep them from doing well.

For one thing, they sometimes think that answers need not be detailed, that long strings of generalities covering the "main ideas" will be adequate. Students may know the details, but since the teacher also knows them, they see no communicative purpose in enumerating specifics. This oversight is compounded when they do not conceive of themselves as strong students and perhaps do not approve of "show-ing off," which is basically what this type of answer requires.

Students often feel, too, that teachers are after some opinion of their own, so that grading essays is very subjective. Therefore, there is no way to study for an essay test. To understand the importance of "psyching out" what a teacher wants, a person need only try answer-ing an essay on a familiar subject but written by an unfamiliar teach-er. It becomes immediately understandable that seemingly factual questions call forth value systems or at least special emphases pe-culiar to a particular teacher. These clues are picked up almost un-consciously by good students, but often completely escape the less adept ones. The problem is that the teachers' assumptions are not al-ways consciously known even to themselves.

Of course, such assumptions are not peculiar to essay tests alone. By the selection and wording of items on an objective test, teachers reveal their own biases. This is not a completely negative or avoidable phenomenon. Part of a student's job, and certainly part of a writer's job, is to make adjustments from audience to audience, to become tolerant of differences and sensitive to expectations. The problem is not that a "hidden curriculum" exists, but that so many teachers (and most students) are unaware of it.

For that reason it is important for students to learn to analyze the questions they are asked on essay tests. Too often students begin answering in response to certain key words they recognize in the test question rather than carefully considering the whole problem—in the context of what has gone on in the class. It helps if there has been an ongoing concern in the classroom for questioning techniques, for distinctions in thinking called forth by differences in words such as "compare" and "illustrate." It behooves the teacher to give careful thought to the wording of questions so that close scrutiny of them is then rewarded.

PREPARING FOR ESSAY TESTS

The best feature of essay tests is the calibre of preparation they require. Because students know they will have to understand implications and draw conclusions, they must review information with this in mind. There can be value in the very uncertainty of the questions to be asked and the knowledge that time will be a problem in answering. These factors can serve as motivation to digest the material and to see trends, connections, and associations otherwise unexamined as the information was presented over a long period of time. Expressive or informal writing will aid in discovering such insights. In short, the kinds of preparation required for essay testing are of a higher order than the kinds of preparation required for objective tests. For a more detailed set of suggestions for studying, see Figure 6.1.

The essay test suggestions in Figure 6.1 are designed for use in any course, since they stress the need to suit the studying to the values and issues raised in class. Most students need practice in converting a reading assignment, a lecture, or an activity into good overview questions. That is why journal writing and small group exercises, such as those described in Chapter 2, are so important. The other hard part about the advice in Figure 6.1 concerns the need to memorize details by writing them as a part of the test preparation. Most students study for essay tests by merely looking at their books and notes rather than by producing the information from scratch in writing. Because

FIGURE 6.1

ADVICE TO STUDENTS ON TAKING ESSAY TESTS

1. Based on your experience of the teacher, brainstorm potential essay questions. This is easier after the first test, of course, but that is sometimes too late. If the teacher hasn't furnished any sample questions, ask for some. From these, brainstorm others, collaborating with other students in the class for even more potential questions.

2. Reword the questions so that they will call for different types of information, using verbs like these:

    compare & contrast   analyze
    discuss   characterize
    explain   cite causes

3. Copy each question onto the top of separate sheets of paper.

4. Go through your notes and textbooks, making lists of specific pieces of information that could be used to support these answers. Write shortened versions of each of these under the questions on the separate sheets of paper.

5. Also make a list of key terms, titles, names, dates, etc.

6. Memorize 4 and 5 above so that a stimulus word will cause you to recall a whole list. Use writing to help you rehearse this.

    It is impossible to stress this enough. Since you
    will be pressed for time during the test itself, you
    must have lots of information at your fingertips.

    Even if your hypothetical questions are not asked, you will have plenty of facts to muster for other questions. You will have confidence because of having learned *too much* to use.

7. Before the test, preferably that same day, take the time to rehearse. This means giving yourself the stimulus words (see 6 above) and actually writing down the lists of data. In your imagination picture yourself in the test room writing. Come to the test already "psyched up" and full of thoughts about the content.

    In doing this you will be pre-writing and reflect-
    ing, activities you don't have time for during the
    essay test period itself.

8. During the test itself, dive right in. Do not worry about being interesting or clever; concentrate instead on clear organization:

    Begin with a sentence which sets you up for parts of an answer: three reasons, five causes, several factors, etc. Then clearly mark the divisions between the parts of your answer, perhaps with separate paragraphs, but certainly with clear transition phrases that tie in with that first sentence. For example:

    The first reason is . . .
    Another cause is . . .
    In addition to the factors . . .

FIGURE 6.1 *(continued)*

ADVICE TO STUDENTS ON TAKING ESSAY TESTS

9. Plan your time. The first question you answer will probably take the longest (just because you aren't into the swing of it yet), but generally allow equal time for each. Remember that you can start with the easiest question rather than the "first" question in order to make sure you do well on the ones you feel you have the best chance on.

10. Think of the whole activity as "showing off"; in the process you may just find your flow of words and your concentration are actually causing you to see new relationships. This most rare of all academic phenomena is called ESSAY TEST HIGH!

---

everything they see looks familiar, they feel they "know it." In actuality they merely recognize it. By way of contrast, the process of writing reinforces learning on several levels: visually, kinesthetically, and mentally. Even though memorized details will not be remembered forever, the process of working with them so closely will cause students to see connections and relationships they would have been unaware of without the intense, disciplined experience of studying this way. This is one more instance of "discovery through writing."

In addition to discussing with students an essay test handout, similar to the one in Figure 6.1, teachers can enhance essay test preparation merely by encouraging lots of other kinds of writing in class. Some suggestions:

- Prepare essay test questions before assigning reading. Then students will have more of an idea what to focus on as they read. Some of the study guides and advance organizers mentioned in Chapter 4 would be appropriate for this approach. Incidentally, the selective retrieval of information discussed in Chapter 5 is also helpful for preparing students to write research papers.
- Have students make up their own questions as part of their informal, written responses to outside reading. These questions can be a regular, continuing assignment in lieu of requiring notes or assigning teacher-made questions. Figure 4.10 describes this activity more fully.
- Let students practice writing an essay answer at home with the promise to observe a twenty-minute time limitation. Some of these answers could be written on ditto for the whole class to read, others simply read aloud, preferably in small groups. Again, it is beneficial for teachers to also join in this activity, perhaps comparing their answer to the students'. If a checklist could be provided to each student, based on the expectations for the answer, then students could in essence grade themselves. Figure 6.2 represents a model

checklist for a question in anthropology. It reflects the advice given in Figure 6.1 in that the answer is supposed to be clearly organized, contain specific details, and use standard writing conventions.

The point is that essay tests should grow out of the rest of the class experience. Indeed, practice in acceptable responses for

---

FIGURE 6.2
_____

A CHECKLIST FOR EVALUATING AN ESSAY ANSWER
IN ANTHROPOLOGY

QUESTION:
What are the physical differences between humans and apes?

DIRECTIONS:
Check each item that holds true for the answer you are evaluating. Then add up the checkmarks to determine a grade according to the point system below.

_____ 1. First sentence gives a hint that the essay answer will be divided into parts (There are four differences, etc.).

_____ 2. Each new part begins with a clear transition (The first difference is, etc.).

_____ 3. *At least three of the following terms are used and spelled correctly:

chimpanzee	primates
gibbon	Anthropoidea
gorilla	Pongidae
orang-utan	Simiidae
anthropoid	Mammal or Mammalia
Metazoa	Hominoidea
Chordata	Hominidae
Vertebrata	Homo sapiens

_____ 4. At least four differences were noted from among these:

mouth	walk on all fours
chin	language
over eyebrows	proportion of arms to legs
top of head	brain size
entrance of backbone to skull	

_____ 5. No faulty information is included or misleading.

_____ 6. Left-out words, sentence errors, misspellings don't amount to more than a total of six.

POINT SYSTEM:
6 – A   3 – D
5 – B   2 }– F
4 – C   1 }

*This item usually separates the A's from the B's.

essays should be part of the classwork from the start through such activities as writing short, spontaneous reactions to new information, preparing class notes, and sharing research reports. Even the small group discussions will help prepare students for essay exams by encouraging questioning and clarifying misconceptions.

DESIGNING ESSAY TESTS

In preparing the tests teachers must be every bit as careful as they would be in designing a research project or any other project that is part of the learning sequence. To avoid confusion about the assumptions behind an essay question, it is useful to become familiar with test design and some system for understanding kinds of intellectual difficulties. Bloom's *Taxonomy of Educational Objectives* offers such a framework.[1] Bloom's idea is that students do not simply know or not know content material. Rather, they come to know it on various levels, beginning with mere recall, progressing through the ability to apply and analyze it, and culminating in the ability to judge its relative worth. The full extent of this hierarchy of cognitive skills is suggested in Figure 6.3, along with key words and sample questions for eliciting responses on these various levels.

In theory, the more advanced stages of cognitive development build on the earlier ones. Thus, a student should not be able to synthesize or integrate material unless he or she can first analyze it or break it into parts. In actuality, however, the categories are not mutually exclusive. A student is often applying a concept in the very process of analyzing it. And, as the sample essay question shows, several levels are often tapped at once. A student who writes a letter in the person of an early Jamestown settler, for example, must be recalling the facts, applying them, and synthesizing them simultaneously. What is important is the realization that effective essay tests assume the lower order skills and call forth the more advanced processes. If they don't, they might as well not be essays.

CREATIVE ESSAY TESTS

If the class has included some game-playing or creative activities, then the essay test situation might be expanded to include more creative tasks. By contriving a rhetorical situation other than student-being-examined, teachers can improve both their own morale and their students'. Once the students get used to the idea, the quality of their answers also improves.

Most of Bloom's cognitive tasks can be adapted to a more personal rhetorical situation. Letters, diary accounts, and persuasive speeches are among the most common of these creative rhetorical situations. Letters can be used to personalize literature, history, and even science by choosing important figures such as Odysseus, Napoleon, or Leeuwenhoek, and having students send a letter about their most recent adventures. Obviously students would have to have more of a

---

FIGURE 6.3

A HIERARCHY OF COGNITIVE SKILLS FOR ESSAY TEST QUESTIONS

1. **Memory:** The student recalls or recognizes information.
   Key terms: Name, define, identify
   Sample question: When did Columbus land in America?

2. **Translation:** The student changes information into a different symbolic form or language.
   Key terms: Explain, describe, tell
   Sample question: How does the water cycle work?

3. **Interpretation:** The student discovers relationships among facts, generalizations, definitions, values, and skills.
   Key terms: Compare, contrast, relate
   Sample question: What is similar about native American Indian culture and tribal African culture?

4. **Application:** The student solves a lifelike problem that requires the identification of the issue and the selection and use of appropriate generalizations and skills.
   Key terms: Show, illustrate, give examples
   Sample question: How do Durkheim's theories of suicide fit the cases cited in *One Flew Over the Cuckoo's Nest?*

5. **Analysis:** The student solves a problem in light of conscious knowledge of the parts and forms of thinking.
   Key terms: Examine, discuss, interpret
   Sample question: Which arguments in *The Federalist Papers* would you interpret as liberal?

6. **Synthesis:** The student solves a problem that requires original, creative thinking.
   Key terms: Suppose, suggest, invent
   Sample question: Given what we know about the moon's surface, what industries might be able to thrive in a moon colony?

7. **Evaluation:** The student makes a judgment of good or bad, right or wrong, according to standards he or she designates.
   Key terms: Criticize, judge, rate
   Sample question: Is it right or wrong to do research on DNA?

Source: The simplification of Bloom's categories with definitions are copied from Norris Sanders, *Classroom Questions: What Kinds?* (New York: Harper and Row, 1966), 3. The key terms and sample questions are original.

sense of setting to do this than they would merely to report Odysseus' wanderings, describe the causes of Napoleon's exile, or to list the steps that led to Leeuwenhoek's invention.

Fictional characters can be invented to filter and interpret content information in mock diaries. Of course, this works best in history where pilgrims can describe the trials of their first winter or aristocrats can describe the concerns of the Elizabethan court. But the technique works equally well for encouraging applications of other content areas—even chemistry or math. A fictional chemist can be locked up with certain chemicals and told to experiment with them to produce ten new substances for fear of losing his life. The student's task is to describe the mixtures he tries. A fictional Everyman can be given a similar "real life problem" to solve in math: calculating gallons of gasoline for a complicated trip or recording probable profits for an enterprise with two or three variables to plan around. It is important to note that the explanations required are of a higher order than merely recording right answers, since they reveal understanding or lack of understanding of processes.

As for persuasive speeches, the possibilities include:

- A politician speaking for or against a given law, using parallel arguments and examples from the U.S. Government textbook
- A behavioral or Freudian psychologist justifying his or her interpretation of a particular case
- King Henry VIII justifying his break with the Roman Catholic Church
- A home economist arguing that all applicants for marriage licenses should study chemistry so as to save money and prevent household accidents
- A character retelling a story from his or her own point of view

Given a certain amount of background, students could also be asked to respond in their own voices, describing and defending the best solutions to specified audiences. For example, students can be asked to present indicators of weather predictions to a local radio station (science); the most economical lengths of lumber to a home builder (math); the best arguments for supporting the United Nations to a congressional committee (political science), and so forth. Here are some additional examples of creative essay test questions with unusual rhetorical contexts:

- *Assume you are a textbook writer. Make up a table of contents for a book on Modern U.S. History.* (This question directs students to outline without their realizing it. A later question could ask for the concluding paragraph of one of those chapters, thus tapping the ability to summarize.)

- *Write a brochure to farmers from the County Farm Extension Worker, explaining scientifically why they can't plant kernels of hybrid corn and get a new crop of hybrid.* (This problem identifies an audience and a purpose while setting up a chance for students to apply their knowledge from biology.)
- *Explain the concept of prime numbers simply enough that even your eight-year-old brother could understand. Be sure to explain why it would be handy to know about prime numbers.* (Again, by establishing a rhetorical context, the test question skirts the awkwardness that occurs when students must explain to their teacher something that they know full well the teacher already knows.)
- *Write a memo to the creator of a familiar TV advertisement as though you were commending him or her for packing in so many psychological gimmicks or hidden persuaders.* (This challenge allows the writer to apply what has been learned about the language and images of advertising to a particular advertisement in a natural way.)

For additional ideas about creative assignments, see Chapter 7.

Each of the above kinds of essays allows the student all the benefits which accrue to the writer of any essay exam: the chance to assimilate materials and to interpret the relationships among discrete pieces of information. By composing the structure and order of the answer, the student is in essence making meaning. What is gained in the innovative essay is, of course, increased interest and motivation. These are two terribly important components of the writing process. In fact, research has shown that spelling and sentence structure improve when even inexperienced students tackle a genuine communication situation.[2] It should be noted, on the other hand, that many older students are initially quite confused by a creative approach to testing. They become so accustomed to "business as usual," especially if not encouraged to develop flexibility as to purpose and audience for writing in English class, that older students must be eased into a sense of confidence about such writing in much the same way that most students need to be eased into accepting small group instruction.

THE PROBLEM OF GRADING

As to the difficulty of grading essay exams, there is only the argument that the pay-offs are worth the effort. Yet there are ways to minimize the drudgery of grading exams while providing students an excellent opportunity to discover and communicate relationships they have perceived in the course material.

In general these difficulties include the time it takes to read everybody's answer; the time it takes to write corrections and comments; and the difficulties of weighing very idiosyncratic essays against an absolute standard. Remembering that most of a student's learning goes on while preparing for and writing the test, teachers would be well advised to invest time in preparing students rather than in responding to what they write. In fact, research shows that most students do not learn much by studying their teacher's corrections and comments.[3]

The best means of assigning grades for essay exams is by means of a checklist derived from the teacher's own dry run with the essay answer or a comparison of good answers with poor answers on past tests. Allowing for trade-offs in emphasis and accuracy, it should be possible to list the traits of an A answer as to length, accuracy, main ideas, and extent of detail expected. Of course, obvious misconceptions, even though irrelevant, would detract from the earned grade. Checklists such as the one in Figure 6.2 can be designed to reflect individual answers and choices within a certain framework. Thus answers to the question comparing men to apes could list various differences and refer to various technical terms but had to contain some details and some evidence of organization. Attention to mechanical errors were also handled in an interesting way on that checklist. Provision was made for some mistakes so that a student had to make six discrete errors to lose a grade. Yet there was no attempt to distinguish between serious and superficial or careless errors.

Although the checklist is easily converted into points, point systems usually reflect an unfortunate attempt to equate essay experience with an objective test. It is difficult to design a point system sensitive enough to reflect the subtle interplay of strengths and weaknesses that characterize most essays. Sometimes a profound insight seems to balance a factual mistake, or an accurate answer might be technically right but too superficial for the full amount of points.

Therefore, experienced teachers may wish to forego the checklist and grade holistically. By this means an intuitive grade is assigned for each essay answer, taking both form and content into account and weighing general strengths against weaknesses. The problem with this method is that it is very easy to be awed by neat handwriting or long answers and to be too punitive against poor spellers, especially as the grader becomes fatigued.

Some teachers go to elaborate lengths not to grade subjectively, say, by grading one answer at a time across tests rather than grading each test separately, by assigning numbers rather than having students use their names, or by adopting a time schedule with frequent breaks. But true objectivity in grading essays is never a very realistic goal since part of the reason for assigning writing is to encourage individual differences. It is not just that information may be right or wrong, but that certain disciplines have characteristic ways of shaping language and individual teachers also have their own idiosyncratic expectations. Adjusting to these is part of the student's job.

Probably the most troublesome aspect of essay grading is what to do about mistakes, either misconceptions about the information or errors in conventions of written English. Correcting such mistakes is of dubious value pedagogically and yet is the most time-consuming part of the evaluation procedure. Hyper-corrections take time and are not the best means of teaching writing anyway. Using editing symbols, including the abbreviation "awk" for awkward or a large question mark for confusing parts of the answer, does not offer much guidance to students for how to avoid such problems. Even counting off a specific amount for specific kinds of errors makes for an unnecessarily cumbersome assessment. Solutions to the problem of evaluating errors include:

- Ignoring errors altogether
- Circling errors for counts
- Using checklists or charts to note error patterns
- Allowing students to revise

In grading holistically the teacher is not looking specifically for errors, but counts off for them to the extent that they interfere with the reader's ability to understand the answer. By simply circling the errors, the teacher has marked them without assuming responsibility for correcting them. Some teachers return essay tests for correction of these errors before giving credit for the grade otherwise earned. Without correction within a specified time limit the test grade reverts to an F.[4] This assumes, of course, that the student can make the corrections by himself or herself, an assumption that may not be viable. If the teacher is interested in supervising error reduction, especially if there is a school-wide writing tutor or handbook, then a standardized checklist, such as the one in Figure 6.2, could be used for all writing assignment in a given course. Teachers should always keep in mind, however, that just because these errors can be easily recognized and explained by experienced writers, they may not be easily eradicated by inexperienced writers.

In any case, teachers should always make clear and content-specific comments on each essay test. This assures the student that the teacher has read the answer. It also serves as a reminder to the teacher of what he or she thought of the answer at the time of grading, should the student later request a private conference to go over the test. Such comments should also help the student understand how to proceed the next time. Some appropriate end comments are:

- Your comment about the use of brackets was confusing since your example contained only parentheses (algebra).
- You apparently confused the terms *meiosis* and *mitosis* (biology).
- By writing so much about the New Deal, you almost ignored the part of the question about the New Frontier (political science).
- The way you explained *mole* more than made up for the mistakes you made in naming elements (chemistry).
- While it's true that many people along the river's edge lied to Huck, it is also true that Huck told lies (literature).

In responding to essay answers teachers should not be discouraged by the initial results. If first test papers are unusually bad in spite of class preparatory activities, then there is all the more reason to persevere.

FIGURE 6.4

SAMPLE CHART FOR RECORDING ERROR PATTERNS

STUDENT'S NAME ———————————————— CLASS ——————————

(To be submitted with each paper or essay test)

Handbook reference	Type of error	Designation of assignment			
	Overall organization				
	Coherence (sticking to point)				
	Paragraph development				
	Sentence structure				
	Comma placement				
	Use of apostrophe				
	Verb forms				
	Pronoun forms				

FIGURE 6.4 (continued)

SAMPLE CHART FOR RECORDING ERROR PATTERNS

Handbook reference	Type of error	Designation of assignment				
	Adjective/adverb forms					
	Parallelism					
	Mismodification					
	Documentation problem					
	Quotation problem					
	Spelling (list words)					
	Other (specify)					

THE "HIDDEN CURRICULUM" AGAIN

Needless to say, teachers' value systems affect their evaluation of answers. Most teachers expect opinions and emphases recorded in essay answers at least to acknowledge their own. Teachers also reveal their attitudes toward language and learning by the way they evaluate essay answers. Teachers who feel that intimidation and punishment are good motivators will tend to write sarcastic comments and assign lower grades. Teachers who feel that support and "positive reinforce-ment" encourage better learning will react to the answers' strengths. Teachers who value objectivity will figure out some type of a point system. Some teachers do not mark the essays at all; others thoroughly edit what students have written. Still other evaluation possibilities will be discussed in Chapter 8.

In order to minimize the extra work all this preparation and follow-through implies, teachers would do well to take changes slow-ly and collaborate with another teacher in the same discipline when thinking through the testing situation and designing class activities. Also, teachers should take all the tests themselves in the same time limit expected of the students so as to be aware of the hidden difficul-ties, both motivationally and cognitively, of the assigned task. From this experience should come a list of expectations for each grade level on particular answers similar to the one in Figure 6.2.

THE PAY-OFFS OF ESSAY TESTS

As has already been mentioned, the best thing about essay testing is the kind of preparation it requires, both as a part of the regular course-work and on the part of individual students studying. A class that encourages questions, demands analysis, and requires proof will lead naturally to the kinds of summing up that essay testing is all about. Students who study by listing facts can muster them more or less auto-matically in subordination of new and complex questions.

There is something challenging to students about knowing that coherent explanations and descriptions will be required. They have additional motivation for writing down their initial informal reactions to new material, knowing they will eventually be required to communicate about the subject in writing. The uncertainty of just what will be asked keeps students looking for trends, connections, and principles and for ideas that will tie together the smaller bits of infor-mation. Thus it is important for students at all levels to know that they will be required to make sense of course material on essay tests.

Students who learn material so well that they can reorder it coherently under pressure are truly in command of the concepts and information of that subject. During the brief, intense time of the test period, various sub-skills of the writing process cannot be the main focus of attention; all skills must be automatically processed in the service of the Almighty Idea. Ironically, then, essay tests represent the least self-conscious of all writing tasks assigned in any course, and, as such, the task most in the content teachers' domain. It is in essay test writing that English truly becomes at once the handmaiden and the tool of the other disciplines.

NOTES

1. Benjamin Bloom, Ed., *Taxonomy of Educational Objectives: Handbook I, Cognitive Domain* (New York: David McKay Co., 1956).

2. See, for example, the discussion in Mina Shaughnessy, *Errors and Expectations* (New York: Oxford University Press, 1977), 85–89.

3. See, for example, discussion in Robert Stiff, "The Effect Upon Student Composition of Particular Correction Techniques," *Research in the Teaching of English* 1 (Spring 1967): 54–75.

4. Idea from Anne J. Herrington, "Writing to Learn: Writing Across the Disciplines," *College English* 43 (April 1981): 386.

7

Creative Writing

School writing, like business writing, is predominantly expository. That is, students and employees are asked most often to describe, explain, or persuade. Those, after all, are the tasks of everyday transactions, the way information is conveyed to get things done. The transactional mode is straightforward, explicit, and factual. Writers in the transactional mode are normally most conscious of the content and organization of their message. They are influenced in the selection and arrangement of material by assumptions about the purpose of the communication and the special needs of the intended readers. When most people think of writing, transactional writing is what they have in mind.

There is, however, another way of writing, springing from different motivation and employing, as it turns out, slightly different mental processes. This writing is sometimes referred to as creative writing to distinguish it from the plainer prose of everyday transactions. Britton calls it "poetic" writing.[1] Poetic writing is not necessarily more private than transactional writing, although it may seem so because its forms are often highly individualistic. A better way to explain the special traits of poetic writing might be to consider it from several angles: its use of language is more self-conscious than transactional prose, its purpose is to delight as well as to inform, and its effect is to create or re-create experience rather than to explain experience. Whereas expository prose is more or less linear (though recursive) in its conception from pre-writing through editing and linear also in its presentation of material, poetic writing works laterally by association in both its conception and its presentation.

Like all good writing, poetic writing balances interpretive generalizations with concrete illustration. The difference is that expository writing alternates these generalities among the illustrations whereas in poetic writing the generalities are embodied rather than embedded.[2] That is, the poetic piece suggests more than it states, whether or not the writer intends such. The embodying of so much meaning is achieved through figurative language, connotations, and the use of symbols that blend subjective meaning into an objectively observable form.

What this means is that the writer of poetic works assumes a different role from that of the transactional writer. In transactional writing the writer is a participant seeking deliberately to accomplish some purpose. In poetic writing the writer is a spectator, suspending "concern with immediate or direct outcomes in order to consider the experience as a whole."[3] Thus poetic writing often achieves a degree of reflection missing in the more practical business of writing and reading expository prose.

In both writing and interpreting poetic pieces, a person maintains a certain aesthetic distance, an awareness that the writing is artistic rather than purely transactional. By being concerned about how a piece is written as well as what it says, the writer is self-consciously a spectator of what he or she writes about.

THE DOMAIN OF POETIC WRITING

Poetic or creative writing tasks have been presented throughout this book. For example, interviews were introduced as an alternative to library resources for the research paper. Simulated diaries and letters were suggested as creative tasks for essay examinations. While there is no clear-cut line between exposition or transactional prose and more imaginative, consciously artistic, poetic writing, there are some distinct differences between the transactional mode in general and the type of writing advocated in this chapter.

The earlier creative tasks were unusual in the specifications of purpose and audience, and, in some cases, in their adoption of a fictional writer other than the student himself or herself. For example, a research paper might be written in the form of a recommendation to be sent to a legislator rather than written as a scholarly treatise and read only by the teacher. Yet transactional tasks are all designed to explain something to somebody for a particular purpose. Thus even very creative expository assignments are merely expansions of the traditional transactional mode, unusual mainly because they are different from most school writing.

By way of contrast, the suggestions in this chapter are not records or reports. Instead, they are more subjective, more reflective, more consciously constructs. Some build on word play, some explore private feelings, some spin fictional webs. Included among these tasks are poems, mottoes, stories, and scripts.

An important realization about poetic constructs, however, is that they, like expository prose, very rarely spring full-blown from brain to paper. Various stages of pre-writing, incubation, drafting, revision, and editing usually precede an accomplished product. In this regard a basic journal or series of expressive writings must precede or accompany production. Indeed, as explained in Chapter 2, expressive writing is the wellspring of all fully developed writing, whether transactional or poetic. The encouragement of poetic pieces is merely the complementary adjunct of the more workaday world of transactional writing.

It is interesting to note that in earlier eras (and, perhaps, quite often even today) the notebooks of scientists and statesmen contained pictures and poems as well as data and explanations—the one form of expression apparently feeding off of and mutually inspiring the other.[4] Thomas Kuhn, in his very provocative book about major scientific breakthroughs, suggests that the creative people responsible for breakthroughs have the capacity to think pictorially, analogically, and symbolically.[5] Another defender of high-level problem-solving also recommends many of the same traits and techniques that would ordinarily seem to be more applicable for poets than for scholars or scientists:

- Overcoming such cultural blocks as the idea that fantasy is a waste of time, that playfulness is only for children, that logic is preferable to intuition
- Establishing an environment where risk-taking, mistakes, incubation periods, and enthusiasm are encouraged
- Practicing deliberate ways of looking at data freshly: modifying, magnifying, minifying, substituting, rearranging, reversing, combining in new ways.[6]

The very same processes exploited in the production of poetic writing are those necessary for mature cognitive development.

OBJECTIONS TO POETIC WRITING

Of course, the main objection to poetic writing is that it is not normally done in courses other than English class. Since most teachers have no experience with encouraging poetic writing, let alone doing it themselves, there seems to be no particular need to begin now. It seems very obvious that expository writing is useful and necessary; creative writing is considered a frill. Like music and athletics, many teachers think poetic writing might be an enjoyable addition to the curriculum but only after the basics were already accounted for. Like music and athletics, too, poetic writing seems to require an expert practitioner as director, not a resident scientist or historian.

Poetic writing, it is admitted, might be enjoyable (for those who like that sort of thing), but it is not thought of as useful. Above all, it is not thought of as contributing to actual learning apart from contributing to some improvement in motivation by keeping students busy.

Even more vehement objections are raised by those who think of creative writing as worse than a frill, who see it as counterproductive to the rigor of academic discipline. Because creative writing is idiosyncratic, they say, it is impossible to teach and difficult to evaluate. With creative writing anything goes. In fact, it can be argued that too much emphasis on creativity in the early grades is what has gotten us into the predicament of declining writing skills in the first place.

Certainly most students lack skill in developing and refining poetic pieces. Without thoughtful instruction, these students are likely to be content with the most vapid productions. They may even view creative writing as child's play. This is a corollary of the idea that poetic writing—more than any other type of writing—springs from talent and inspiration, which is simply not available to everybody.

For all of these reasons many teachers consider creative or poetic writing to be outside of their domain. Hard pressed even to incorporate more traditional writing into their coursework, they see no reason whatsoever for attempting to promote creativity through poetic writing.

THE VALUE OF POETIC WRITING

Actually, poetic writing is very often an expression of greater depth and texture than occurs in transactional accounts. The sounds of the words, the connotations evoked, the symbols manipulated—whether deliberately or naively—communicate to a different set of expectations than expository writing does.

A simplified way of defending poetic writing is to suggest that it uses more of the brain than expository writing does. Much has been written about the hemispheric functions of the brain, about the dominance of the left hemisphere in our traditional measurement of academic learning.[7] The left hemisphere is supposedly the center of writing; it is rational, linear, focusing on the parts of the whole. The right hemisphere is supposedly the aural center; it is analogical, emotional, focusing on the whole rather than the separate parts. Although all people use both halves of the brain, since these are, of course, intricately interconnected, many critics agree that exaggerated left-hemispheric dominance is unsatisfying emotionally and limiting cognitively.[8]

In using more of the brain, more avenues to or layers of perception and expression, the writer of poetic constructs is more fully and personally involved in the task at hand. A poem, such as the one written in Figure 7.1, concretizes an abstract concept and sets up for both reader and writer a visual and aural association. Since all language is symbolic anyway, and much of it is metaphorical, poetic writing is really only an exaggeration of the ordinary functions of language. That exaggeration—whether through conciseness, analogy, or sensory evocation—calls attention to itself and thus expresses more and communicates more than ordinary language does.

The kinds of learning which accrue exclusively from poetic writing complement and balance the generally more measurable learning communicated in transactional writing. By the same token, poetic writing cannot replace the need for expository prose in content courses. Its strong points are mainly, though not exclusively, affective:

1. Poetic creations stimulate greater attention both to details and to abstract concepts. They also stimulate a more complete integration of private and public experience.
2. Poetic creations evoke insights by stimulating aural, visual, or figurative representations of factual material.
3. Poetic creations, by their individualistic character, are nonquantifiable and thus eliminate the negative aspects of artificial competition in the classroom.
4. Poetic creations represent the highest levels of Bloom's taxonomy[9] by allowing students to imagine applications of material that translate objective data into highly personal syntheses.
5. Poetic creations satisfy an apparent human need for aesthetic beauty and playfulness, thus satisfying students on a deeper level than other writing and testing situations afford.

Interestingly enough, creative writing seems to thrive whenever genuine inquiry is encouraged within the classroom.[10] Just as learning is best induced by encouraging active questioning, so too is poetic writing. Good learning and good writing are both encouraged by open questioning, focused attention, mastery of a knowledge base, expanding concepts, and divergent thinking.

HOW TO USE POETIC WRITING

In content courses, only rarely can poetic writing be the sole writing encouraged. Extensive coaching or large expenditures of class time for poetic writing also would be inappropriate in most content courses. A more realistic approach comes from a three-pronged encouragement of creativity:

1. Surrounding students with displays of relevant poetic writing by other students and by professionals
2. Encouraging poetic writing in class activities that introduce students to short, creative tasks
3. Offering choices on large projects that allow some students to fulfill requirements poetically

Each of these approaches will be explored more fully below.

Displays

Besides mentioning titles and occasionally reading from books of poetry or fiction, teachers should keep examples of relevant creative writing and drawings constantly in view: on classroom bookshelves, bulletin boards, and display areas. This encourages extra-curricular reading while establishing an atmosphere of inquiry. The displayed items also serve as inspiration and indirect models for student writing.

For titles of creative pieces appropriate to the different disciplines, teachers should check back issues of their trade journals or indexes of *English Journal* and *College English* for articles about reading done in interdisciplinary courses. A teacher's own favorites are also usually appropriate. Historical fiction and science fiction not only provide creative stimulation, but encourage interest in the subject matter of the course as well.

Whenever copies of private notebooks kept by famous scholars or inventors are available, these, too, should be displayed, especially when they contain drawings and schematics as well as words. Arthur Koestler, in *The Act of Creation*, offers numerous examples of creative discoveries recorded in the notebooks of such famous scientists and mathematicians as Albert Einstein, Henri Poincaré, and Jacques Hadamard.[11] Displays of such pages legitimize the free-wheeling, exploratory interconnections among ideas and approaches that accompany all creative ventures.

In fact, displays which illustrate analogical thinking should predominate. Examples would be photographs, blue-prints, or art work on similar themes, such as the construction of organic cells or aerial views of the earth. Visual materials make more effective displays, but some examples of student writing should also be included.

Analogies

Analogies are extended comparisons of words or ideas from entirely different realms of experience. Analogies bridge the gap between logic and intuition, between exposition and creative writing. If cars are compared to dinosaurs, that is an analogy. If cars are compared to trucks, however, that is merely a comparison (or contrast) and not an analogy. The words or ideas under scrutiny in an analogy must represent an unlikely link, a link from different classifications.

For the purposes of encouraging discovery through writing, students have to move beyond knowing how analogies work and recognition of valid analogies to the creation of analogies and particularly to the writing of extended lists of similarities among items being compared. The mind seems to want to do this, to think analogically. Many words and phrases are analogical without our being conscious of it. The phrase "I see" can mean "I understand," for example, and is immediately interpreted literally although it is really an analogy in metaphorical form. To be conscious of the implicit metaphorical nature of language is indeed the first step toward appreciating and creating artistic writing. Most poems are based on the analogical process.

What analogies accomplish cognitively is an isolation of relevant features and the recombination of information to exaggerate certain of these features. The ability to make distinctions among parts of a whole is the first step toward the ability to analyze, one of Bloom's more advanced cognitive skills.[12] Furthermore, by extending the points of similarity in an analogy, students are probing to discover insights. The analogy, after all, is only valid if it can be extended. Thus, an analogy between a star and human eye is invalid if the only point of comparison is that both shine. An analogy between a star and the sun is invalid because they both belong to the same classification: both are stars. An analogy between an eye and a camera, however, is valid because it can be developed in an extended way: the lens, the variable opening, the reverse focusing of the image.

In standard format, such an analogy would look like this:

camera : shutter : : eye : eyelid

It is read, "Camera is to shutter as eye is to eyelid." The first and third terms of the analogy must be parallel, as must be the second and fourth. The relationship between the first two terms (in this case, the overall object to its smaller part) must also be the same as the relationship between the second two. There are many other analytical relationships possible among terms of analogies (object to trait of the object, object to function, one part of speech to another part of speech, etc.). This very multiplicity of possible relationships and the succinct reduction inherent in the four-word format of analogies make them popular objective test items.[13]

It is sometimes fun, in fact, to discover breakdowns in analogies, which are often not so much inaccuracies as the subordination of objective fact to serve a more subjective kind of truth: the truth about an experience expressed. Figure 7.1 represents a poem based on an extended analogy, the biological part of which has been subordinated to make a point about human intelligence. In Figure 7.1, a spider spinning its web is analogous to a human intelligence making sense of the world. The analogy is extended: both are forms of making connections, both originate from the creature and reach out to the environment, both are continuous activities, both are fragile operations. Yet the description of how a spider spins its web—the word *spin* itself is a metaphor—is subordinated to the overall philosophical truth. This poem is really not about spiders at all, but about an inquisitive approach to life, the human desire to make meaning.

Students often need help in appreciating the complexities of objective truth, scientific truth, and subjective, personal truth. Studying analogies and then poems built on analogies can promote inquiry into these kinds of philosophical distinctions. Other ways to use analogies in class include having small groups brainstorm analogies which explain certain key concepts; having students write poems *or* explanations on the basis of furnished four-word analogies (such as the one comparing cameras and eyes); asking students to create analogies in their four-word form from textbook explanations built on analogies (but not always readily recognizable as such without careful study); and taking an analogy from one student's expressive writing and asking other students to respond to it in a freewriting activity prior to a class discussion.

Labels

Another "bridge" activity between straight exposition and the more poetic activity of writing slogans or mottoes (described below) is to have students work with labels. Labels are simply short descriptive phrases which summarize a concept or experience, coalesce abstractions, or focus relationships. They name charts, illustrations, cartoons, or whole displays by articulating what is implied or what the parts of the whole have in common. Creating labels can be the task of groups completing projects, such as models of geological layers of earth or charts reporting the results of voting patterns. Creating labels for political cartoons or photographs of biological processes can be part of a competitive game designed to sharpen ability to make inferences or observations. Removing labels from charts or graphs in math class can set up an inductive reasoning task for individuals or small groups.

Obviously students must understand the information pictured before they can write appropriate labels. Labeling is thus the ultimate

FIGURE 7.1

A NOISELESS PATIENT SPIDER

by Walt Whitman (1881)

A noiseless patient spider,
I mark'd where on a little promontory it stood isolated,
Mark'd how to explore the vacant vast surrounding,
It launch'd forth filament, filament, filament, out of itself,
Ever unreeling them, ever tirelessly speeding them.

And you O my soul where you stand,
Surrounded, detached, in measureless oceans of space,
Ceaselessly musing, venturing, throwing, seeking the spheres to connect them,
Till the bridge you will need be form'd, till the ductile anchor hold,
Till the gossamer thread you fling catch somewhere, O my soul.

Source: From Harold W. Blodgett and Sculley Bradley, Eds. *Leaves of Grass* (New York: W.W. Norton and Company, 1965), 450.

---

summarizing activity. Labels are fun to create and useful in the way they attract attention. They can also contribute to provocative classroom displays. Since students must be able to create labels or abstractions for many ordinary, transactional writing tasks—for example, writing main headings for outlines, naming reports, deriving arguments for persuasive papers—labeling has obvious "useful" applications. On the other hand, labels can be fanciful or metaphorical, especially when they are naming cartoons or illustrations, so the labeling activity is also a first step toward more poetic enterprises.

Mottoes and Slogans

Slogans and mottoes are the creative counterpart of labels. They capture imaginatively and concisely the principle of an activity, experience, or concept. Slogans and mottoes are really one-sentence or one-phrase summaries. They can apply to cities, people, historical events, or by personification to inanimate objects or processes. Often they are playful twists of advertising slogans, clichés, or folk proverbs. Alliteration and puns are encouraged. And they are contagious. One or two eager youngsters, following the teacher's lead, will soon plaster the classroom with mottoes and slogans for every part of the class experience. Figure 7.2 presents some samples.

Slogans are fun to create; they represent artistic self-consciousness in building on factual knowledge; and they suggest more than they literally state. The slogan about Marie Antoinette, for instance, rests on knowledge of her legendary statement about letting the peas-

FIGURE 7.2

SAMPLE SLOGANS

FAMOUS PEOPLE
James Watt (the inventor): He got into hot water!
Marie Antoinette: Well bread, she lost her head!
Houdini: You'll wonder where the fellow went!

PLACES
Amsterdam: Reflections of cheerful practicality
The Ohio River: Mid-America's liquid conveyor belt
The moon: Often seen, but never heard

OBJECTS
The Santa Maria: Three sheets to the wind
Gutenberg Press: Germany's ticket to the Reformation
Pigs: Little pink elephants traveling without their trunks

EVENTS
Martin Luther King's Assassination: The King is dead; long live the dream!
The Wright Brothers' Flight: Orville sat in the catbird seat!
The Civil War: When the U.S. bruised itself gray and blue

PROCESSES
The Scientific Method:
Nature's answer to chance
Guess, Test, Express
An ounce of prevention is worth a pound of care

WORKS OF LITERATURE
The Scarlet Letter:
Hester really knew how to make A's
Dimmesdale's sins were unseenly
He who least laughs lasts (Chillingworth)

LANGUAGE
Punctuation: When in doubt, leave it out
Spelling: Rites of right writing
Upper case letters: Capital ideas stand out

---

ants eat cake if they have no bread. The slogan for Amsterdam rests on the knowledge that Amsterdam is a city of canals and tradesmen. The slogan for the Wright brothers rests on a pun about Kitty Hawk.

Teachers who use the same classroom all day can encourage ongoing production of mottoes and slogans on a large sheet of paper serving as a kind of graffiti board. As in all other kinds of writing, the ongoing production of writing on this board creates other ideas and stimulates more writing of the same sort.

Poems

Once analogical thinking and word play are introduced, it is a very small step to encourage the writing of poetry. Although many techniques and exercises can be incorporated into the formal study of poetry in an English class, the content teacher will want to minimize preoccupation with form and concentrate instead on two aspects of writing poetry: the extended metaphor using information and experiences from course activities, and the expression of subjective feeling inspired by that information and those experiences.

Teachers of math or social studies or science are unlikely to give up class time for discussions of rhyme or meter. Yet they might be open to preliminary expressions of the poetic muse which show up in their students' expressive writing, record-keeping, or conversation. David Holbrook gives many examples of such sensitivity among teachers in response to notes taken by British school children on field trips.[14] On one occasion a boy recorded measurements, described weather conditions, and listed equipment taken on a trip up a mountain. On a postcard home he revealed that several climbers had earlier been killed at that place. Tucked in among this objective data was one sentence about the teacher scrambling down after a fallen mitt. Quite possibly the experience of watching that mitt fall had called forth some unrecorded fear, a description of which would be more appropriate in poetry than in a traditional report written about the trip. A teacher responding to the notes could have encouraged the boy to write a poem about the falling mitt, thereby integrating that student's personal perception with an externally observable event. In fact, whenever close observation, first-hand experience, or emotionally charged information is part of the coursework, poetry is an appropriate response.

Students need not be concerned with lots of rules for writing poetry, especially when both professional and student-written examples are readily observable and occasionally read in the classroom. As teachers personally experiment with poetry-writing, however, they may come to feel that certain prescribed forms are indeed worthy of being introduced to and elicited from the class. Haiku and quintains are typical of the many prescribed forms which might seem particularly suitable for certain courses.

Haiku, with their three-line, seventeen-syllable limitation, are appropriate for science classes because they rely on concrete sensory details to suggest a feeling. Figure 7.3 is an example of a classical haiku of the sort which might be appropriate for display. Figure 7.3, like many haiku, uses only phrases rather than complete sentences. It suggests, but does not directly state, an appreciation of the unity

FIGURE 7.3
_____

A CLASSICAL HAIKU

> The beginning of fall:
> the ocean, the rice fields—
> one green for all!

of nature, and it does this through description of a direct observation. Students can be encouraged to create haiku as part of field trips in natural settings or in response to movies which evoke sensory impressions second-hand. If more "scientific" records are also kept, the two kinds of writing can be displayed side-by-side and discussed for their differences.

In contrast to haiku, quintains require logic rather than intuition to produce. Here playfulness and originality count for more than deeply felt emotion. Still, the exercise can provoke insights as it requires writers to consider a topic in multiple ways. Quintains are written in five lines of one or two words each: the first line a noun, the second two traits (adjectives), the third a feeling, the fourth an action, and the fifth a synonym. Figure 7.4 is an example of a quintain. Quintains like the one in Figure 7.4 are appropriate in any class which introduces specialized vocabulary. Teachers can list a few nouns which might be used for first lines, then let individual students or groups of students fill in the rest. Some examples of first lines: *neuroses* in psychology, *erosion* in earth science, *Napoleon* in history, *calisthenics* in physical education. Quintains also make good responses to stories in English class as a character's name, traits, and actions can be drawn out of each student, then compared among students in small groups.

Poetic creations—whether haiku, quintains, or some other form—are pleasurable complements to the more traditional transactional writing usually expected in non-English courses. Quite surprisingly, poetic works can also promote learning of factual data, particularly of data requiring an organizational concept for its retention. Apparently just by working through the intricate relationships of an extended metaphor, students come to understand in a deeper, more complete way.

Figure 7.5 is poetry not because it rhymes or manifests other poetic techniques, but simply because it is a suggestive piece arrived at consciously by expanding a comparison between locks and molecules as a means of explaining enzyme action. From it the writer came to understand the concept of the *active site* where only a specific enzyme works for its substrate. Poetry promoted cognitive development.

FIGURE 7.4

A QUINTAIN FOR ALGEBRA

A QUINTAIN FOR ALGEBRA

Equations—
Balanced, logical—
I puzzle and fret,
Swapping factors—
Equivalents.

FIGURE 7.5

SAMPLE POEM

A Substrate with a Secret

Not every enzyme I confront
Will unlock the confines of my heart—
Only those with special keys
Spark reactions of their sort
Within the secret tumblers of me.

Source: Based on the *Lock and Key Hypothesis* as one way of explaining enzyme action as described in Raymond F. Oram, Paul J. Hummer, and Robert C. Smoot, *Biology: Living Systems.* 3rd ed. (Columbus, Ohio: Merrill, 1979), 92–93.

Translations from Another Mode

Translating written language into another representation or vice versa rearranges information in such a way as to evoke startling insights. The student doing this is internalizing the patterns inherent in the stimulus and converting them to an entirely different form. This is a deeper internalizing process than merely converting one verbal form into another, yet it is good preparation for that because it allows the student to assume control.

The most common "translation" activity is the conversion of words into rough pictures. Not only must spatial relationships be understood for translations to be possible, but the process of the translating forces the relationships into understanding. This process has already been discussed as an avenue to assessment in Chapter 3 and as an intermediate activity between record-keeping and analyzing in Chapter 4. There the translations were presented, in such exercises as converting charts into words, as part of the skill needed for transactional writing. Here the concern is with a different kind of learning: the deeper, more personal creation of meaning that comes in poetic writing when associations and suggestions are consciously extended for their own sakes.

Since the purpose is not to encourage drawing or painting for their own sakes, legitimate as that goal may be as yet another offshoot of content learning, this chapter suggests writing assignments that derive from visual stimuli rather than the other way around. Films and photographs are especially conducive to the kinds of free associating that prefigures poetic creations. These can be shown in class to inspire the personal involvement that could spark mottoes, short poems, or prose pieces. Although not every student would be expected to refine these associations, each could benefit from the lists of images, feelings, and connections with earlier learnings and the synergism of sharing these lists and adding to them in small group exchanges. Figure 7.6 represents an in-class list of associations written in response to a photograph of a funerary head from Ghana in an anthropology class. The student whose list is presented was asked to extend one observation in greater detail. This activity caused the student to look more closely at the artifact and also to draw out implications related to information given in class. The next step could easily be a poetic creation celebrating the mournful quality that the student focused on in her extended observation.

Given the stimulus of constant exposure to displays of artistic productions and practice in pre-writing such pieces, some students will eventually be drawn to more fully realized pieces of poetic writing. Occasionally students' motivation to complete these projects may justify the substitution of a creative project for one more typical of academic assignments, such as the research paper. A close monitoring of student journals and short in-class productions may identify those who could learn more from developing science fiction stories, poems, plays, or short stories than from expository prose. Below are some specific projects, themselves suggestive of others, which would involve students emotionally because of their concreteness and adaptations of information into the terms of human experience.

Stories

Stories could include dialogue and plot or merely describe a particular situation, as in a vignette. Such productions are particularly appropriate in the social sciences where case studies are accepted expressions

FIGURE 7.6

LIST OF ASSOCIATIONS BASED ON A FUNERARY HEAD FROM GHANA

all features drooping
ears like discs sticking out low
mouth open as though saying "Oh"
eyelids half closed
eyes slanting down at outside
    edges as though crying
brow either frowning or scarred
flat cheeks

The stylized face seems to convey
sadness - all the features droop down, an
effect exaggerated by how low the ears are
(This face could never wear glasses
because the top of the ear is lower than
needed for earpieces). The eyebrows are
just a slightly curved line parallel to
the curve of the mouth below, which seems
to be rounded into a shape for moaning
(saying "Oh"). I guess all this sadness
is because of death since it's a funerary
head.

Source: Pictured in Howard Hibbard, The Metropolitan Museum of Art (New York: Harper and Row, Publishers, 1980), 573.

of general principles, with each case representing a type and hence suggesting more than it literally conveys. Adaptations of historical themes or illustrations of social dilemmas would be appropriate for this type of project. These would be fairly realistic, though emitting the suggestiveness of recurring images or connotations and other literary devices the way all fiction does.

Other stories might be even more deliberately artifacts: stories about the water cycle told from the point of view of a rock, or a lab report written in the form of a mystery.[15] Each is in its own way an extension of empathy with the possibilities new information presents; each, therefore, is a way of overcoming the egocentricity that mars much immature writing.

There are many problems inherent in writing fiction, however, and most students will have considerable difficulty in developing natural dialogue, building suspense, and sustaining humor. Indeed, most older students would have to take a creative writing course to develop adequate expertise in effective narration. Without special training, most would write only the mere outline of an effective story. For these reasons longer projects should probably not be required of all students, but merely encouraged or allowed among those who seem already to be good at writing them by virtue of wide reading or a habit of story-writing carried over from earlier years.

People of all ages are naturally attracted to narrative form and would probably write more narratives if encouraged continously from early childhood. The writing of narratives, in fact, is one of those tasks which best illustrate the spiral nature of writing development. Young students write stories naturally as an extension of play. Students at various ages and with varying experiences in reading fiction can return to the writing of narratives with an ever-increasing repertoire of techniques. Professional writers spend their lifetimes perfecting the art of storytelling.

For the purpose of this book all that needs reiterating is the possibility that some students, who are more imaginative or less drawn to the role of "detached scholar" than their peers, may learn more from writing extended poetic works than they would from half-heartedly attempting more traditional papers. The added involvement may even spark their interest (and that of their peers) in the subject matter of the course. Once involved, a student may do well in the course and even pursue the discipline later because of the good feelings engendered by being given the opportunity to do a poetic piece of writing.

Documentaries, Plays, and Skits

In any class there are materials for documentaries, films, or radio shows, the scripts of which could be written to introduce the general public to controversies inherent in course material or imaginary interviews with historic people. A TV skit could dramatize the controversies which characterized the Constitutional Convention, for example. Futuristic scenarios could detail the long-term results of present trends in pollution.

One teacher[16] has his students write dialogues explaining certain concepts in science. The dialogues are between a science specialist and an announcer. They are aimed at average people unfamiliar with the concepts. For that audience the writer must understand information well enough to explain it convincingly. These students go a step further, however, and actually submit their manuscripts to commercial radio stations, thus adding a dimension of realism to their assignment.

Plays and skits can be used in a similar way. Students can explore a hypothetical situation, using the fuller development of imaginative characters and settings as a vehicle for expanding their own experience and that of their readers (or hearers or viewers). The play or skit can be written to give information as well as pleasure.

THE EVALUATION OF POETIC WRITING

Most poetic writing should be responded to in ways other than direct grading. Since poetic writing is the most innately satisfying of all forms of writing, it represents the perfect opportunity for other forms of response: displaying it, sharing it in small groups, reading it aloud to the whole class, publishing it. (Each of these with the writer's permission, of course.) Publishing can mean sending it off for consideration to a national publisher, entering it in a local contest, reproducing it for distribution within a class, or having individual students assemble their piece of writing into a hand-made book of their own.[17] Such responses carry with them the natural reward of recognition; also the built-in motivation for quality control that public recognition implies.

Teachers who do assign grades for pieces of poetic writing will soon find themselves in a double bind. On the one hand, there is the chance of hurting students' feelings by harshly judging something they have a personal stake in. On the other hand, there is a lack of critical standards implied by giving everything the grade of A. Preferable to either of these alternatives is the option of giving "credit" for the completion of poetic writing rather than assigning it a particular grade. Normally there are enough other grades in a term's work that an average can be determined without judging the poetic writing.

When students are used to receiving grades for everything they do—or when they are unaccustomed to doing poetic writing and hence not willing to take it seriously—teachers may have to give definite "credit" as a motivator for making sure poetic tasks receive the attention they deserve.

Perhaps the best way to offer credit for pieces such as analogies, mottoes, or short poems is to set up point systems and give a set number of points for the completion of certain poetic assignments. One way to do this is to specify the traits required of a piece for credit. A four-word analogy, for example, must have passed the scrutiny of peer group evaluation to make sure that both halves of the analogy are consistently related. Or a poem submitted for credit must have exploited a metaphor (if that was the challenge put forth in the directions). There might also be specifications for correcting spelling or rewriting the pieces neatly before credit is awarded. If the course grade for the term is based on a point system, then a set percentage of those points might be assigned to poetic tasks, the students deciding for themselves which tasks to do to fulfill the requirement.

For extended poetic works, such as more complicated poems or short stories, the teacher might want to set up individualized criteria for grading. This would be particularly appropriate if the extended piece is to substitute for a research paper or some other traditional assignment. By meeting with the student early in the composing process and "drawing out" the poetic piece in conference, the teacher can negotiate criteria particular to a given project. For instance, if a student of math has shown an interest in writing a play to dramatize concrete ways of solving word problems, the grade might be based on the length of the script, the number of examples depicted in the play, the effectiveness of revisions made after the play had been rehearsed, actual performance of the play, and the looks of the edited manuscript. However, even when a poetic project accounts for a large percentage of the work of a course, the teacher may choose to award credit rather than assign a grade. As has already been mentioned, this can be done by simply averaging the other grades. If the poetic project is especially good or noticeably shabby, the term grade could be raised or lowered by one grade.

More important than the awarding of credit or a grade to a finished poetic product, though, is the response given it in other ways. Context-specific comments—both oral and written—are very important in responding to poetic pieces. Teachers should take care to single out those parts of the piece which really communicate and tell why. Mentioning strengths is much more important than pointing out weaknesses whenever poetic endeavor is being nurtured. In fact, any pointing out of weaknesses should be done by way of questioning either by a peer or by the teacher while the work is still in process rather than after it is finished. For instance, after hearing the rough draft of a short story about hybernation told from the point of view of a bear, students in a response group might ask for more details about the setting or clues that would make clear the species of the bear.

What seems obvious in considering ways of evaluating poetic writing is that great care must be taken to treat the tasks differently from normal transactional pieces. Because creativity is inspired by associational linking and intuition, it requires a supportive environment where risk-taking is encouraged rather than punished. Just as the production of poetic pieces is personal, so the response to them must be.

THE PAYOFFS OF POETIC WRITING

Many teachers inadvertently stifle the creative or poetic in themselves and in their students and retain very little interest in encouraging it. Those who do enjoy reading fiction or writing poetry often think of their interest as recreational and certainly as irrelevant to the learning situation in their own discipline. Yet recent research has supported the claim that artistic expression does affect cognitive development. This seems to be true for various reasons:

1. The poetic mode is more innately satisfying because it imitates a fuller range of human experience and allows associations and sensory impressions to determine its shape.
2. The poetic mode extends normal first-hand experience by setting up a vicarious substitute, thereby promoting empathy and reducing egocentrism.
3. The poetic mode explores and communicates relationships among individual words and longer rhetorical units metaphorically; in so doing it suggests more than it literally states, delighting its author and readers by means of this challenge.
4. The poetic mode is accessible to inexperienced and minority students who are unfamiliar with or uncomfortable with academic prose.
5. Creativity sparks involvement and promotes a good attitude (and pride) toward writing.

Creative writing is thus a good antidote to the dominant assumption of science about the world, an assumption that by extension permeates the whole of the academic establishment. The assumption is that reality is "out there." Through writing, and particularly through poetic writing, however, people participate in the construction of reality. After all, "Man is an analogist and studies relations in all objects."[18] Only through art is man made conscious of what transpires whenever imagination is at work on raw material. In the words of Jerome Bruner:

> Once we have coded experience into language, we can (but not necessarily do) read surplus meaning into the experience of pursuing the built-in implications of the rules of language.[19]

Poetic writing reads that surplus meaning into experience.

James Moffett is even more eloquent in his plea for encouraging creative writing across the curriculum. Moffett feels that not only would individual students benefit from a more comprehensive approach to writing, but that our society as a whole would be more satisfying if our schooling was not so one-sided. In his words:

> An overemphasis of the verbal/analytic half of the brain in our own culture is endangering the culture because it drives out the integrative, analogical thinking desperately needed to coordinate action within the vast intricacies of both individual and international life in this era of modern technology. Balance is the key, and the grand paradox is that people reason and verbalize better if they stop sometimes in favor of intuition and metaphor.[20]

NOTES

1. James Britton et al., *The Development of Writing Abilities, 11–18* (Urbana, Illinois: National Council of Teachers of English, 1975).

2. This distinction made by James Moffett, *A Student-Centered Language Arts Program, K–13* (Boston: Houghton Mifflin Co., 1968), 441.

3. Arthur N. Applebee, "Writing Across the Curriculum: The London Projects," *English Journal* 66 (December 1977): 82.

4. See Arthur Koestler, *The Act of Creation* (New York: Dell, 1967).

5. See Thomas Kuhn, *The Structure of Scientific Revolutions* (Chicago: The University of Chicago Press, 1965).

6. Ideas adapted from James Adams, *Conceptual Blockbusting* (San Francisco: W.H. Freeman, 1974).

7. See summary in Janet Emig, "Writing as a Mode of Learning," *College Composition and Communication* 28 (May 1977): 122–128.

8. Moffett, pp. 461–462.

9. Benjamin Bloom, Ed., *Taxonomy of Educational Objectives: Handbook I, The Cognitive Domain* (New York: David McKay Co., 1972).

10. Edna DeHaven, "A Questioning Strategy Model for Creative Writing," *Elementary English* 50 (September 1973): 959–961, 987.

11. Koestler, pp. 114–185.

12. Bloom, *op. cit.*

13. For a fuller explanation of how analogies work, see Hugh P. O'Neill, S.J., *Reasoning by Analogy* (Detroit: University of Detroit Press, 1967).

14. David Holbrook, *Children's Writing: A Sampler for Student Teachers* (Cambridge, England: University Press, 1967). See particularly pp. 63–64.

15. This suggestion came from the English Methods class of Peter Schiff, Northern Kentucky University.

16. John Wilkes, Lecturer in Science Writing at the University of Southern California, Santa Cruz, mentioned in Stephen Judy and Susan Judy, *An Introduction to the Teaching of Writing* (New York: John Wiley, 1981), 81.

17. Idea adapted from Christopher Parry, *English Through Drama: A Way of Teaching* (Cambridge, England: University Press, 1967), 212–213.

18. Owen Barfield, *Poetic Diction* (Middletown, Connecticut: Wesleyan Press, 1973), 92.

19. Jerome Bruner quoted in Britton, p. 204.

20. Moffett, p. 461.

8

Evaluation of Student Writing

Of all the components of a writing program, probably none is more important than how pieces of writing are evaluated. Evaluation, of course, can mean many things: judgment of relative worth, match with specified criteria, identification of strengths and weaknesses, responding to the purpose of the writing (being entertained, implementing a suggestion, penning a reply, etc.). And every stage of the writing process is influenced by a writer's view of the reader's eventual response. As has already been mentioned, writer's block is largely caused by fear of criticism, even self-criticism inflicted by censoring words and ideas before they are written down. Students whose early drafts are not going to be responded to at all may very well by-pass the early, messy stages of writing and opt for a commercially produced paper which is error-free and beyond reproach.

Yet students have built up certain expectations about how teachers should and will respond to their papers. Their expectations in this regard very much affect the way they write and the way they feel about writing. Too much deviation from these expectations will cause anxiety even when past experience with teacher response has been unpleasant. What students have come to expect all too often from their teachers is a search for errors and a preference for length and verbosity.[1] Without detailing yet another discussion of the harm done to the cause of writing and learning from premature emphasis on abstraction and accuracy without commensurate attention to pre-writing and revision, suffice it to say that traditional grading practices often stifle improvement in writing.

Because of the way their papers have been and will be evaluated, students are often stymied. They either work too hard for meagre results or procrastinate, dreading both the writing task and the ultimate reckoning of the grade on that task. In fact, there is considerable evidence that fear of writing (which is actually fear of being exposed through writing) affects career choice, with especially anxious writers choosing careers they judge not to require writing.[2] The same fear probably also contributes to the spread of plagiarism.

To look at options in evaluating student writing is to challenge many assumptions about language and about learning.

ASSUMPTIONS ABOUT EVALUATION

Rarely do we examine our assumptions about student writing. Most teachers presume that the purpose of evaluating student writing is to judge it good or bad against set standards, offering such comments and criticism as will justify the grade and prevent similar mistakes or oversights in future papers. Error is the focus of traditional evaluations of student papers, and various studies on what teachers look for reveal remarkably similar criteria and methods of response.[3]

Another issue in evaluating writing concerns the expectation of ideal performance. Content teachers often expect more than their students are able to produce, not only as to ideas and organization, but also as to spelling and other conventions of writing. Specifying one's expectations is, of course, no guarantee that students can match them. This is not to say that content teachers should lower standards or accept mediocrity. But through experience and assessment all teachers should develop awareness of what students in a particular place can produce. And they should recognize the developmental processes by which a student progresses in skill and decide which salient features of writing can be isolated for specialized attention in the evaluation process.

PROBLEMS WITH EVALUATION

Research reveals that most students do not pay much attention to teachers' comments on their papers.[4] If there are grades on the papers as well as comments, students will look for the grade and ignore the comments. And for good reason: the comments are often illegible, the abbreviations and proofreading symbols misunderstood, and the advice contradictory. Often, for example, the same paragraph in a paper may draw comments about the need to explain more and, at the same time, request corrections on punctuation. The first comment indicates a need for revision while the second assumes the paper is ready for editing. If the paper is finished, it is too late to make any changes called for in the comments. There are other reasons, too, why students normally disregard their teachers' comments. The comments often concern mechanics and form; presumably such comments could be affixed to any paper, regardless of content. Rare are content-specific comments which reflect the teacher's careful reading of what was said, of the information conveyed. Students thus sense that their teacher has not paid attention to the communication when the comments concern form and mechanics instead of content. The grade, rather than the communication, becomes the focus of attention.

Figure 8.1 illustrates typical teacher responses to a page of student writing. The teacher's comments illustrate many of the problems already noted. Students would be confused about the question mark and the abbreviation "awk" for "awkward sentence." They might not recognize what had offended the teacher. Furthermore, the corrections seem appropriate for different stages of the writing process. The spelling correction assumes that the student is ready to edit whereas the call for more information presumes the revising stage. In all, the comments seem curiously unrelated to this particular paper: they could have been attached to any paper. The student is left wondering whether the teacher really read the paper at all or whether, in fact, only the form and mechanics matter.

One reason for the tradition of heavily edited markings on student papers may have little to do with pedagogy at all. Errors are circled and underlined by the teacher not so much to help students as to reveal that the teacher has noticed. Nothing is easier for the experienced reader to spot than mechanical errors. But just because errors are easily spotted does not mean they can be easily corrected. A good example is that most common of errors, the sentence fragment. Easy to spot. Hard to eradicate. Without some understanding of the developmental processes natural in the acquisition of writing skill, it is almost impossible, in fact, to set baseline expectations on the mechanics of writing. The important point is not to confuse "first thing noticed" by the teacher as synonymous with "first thing the student should fix."

There is an art to marking student papers deliberately rather than automatically. The art has not so much to do with the overall evaluation of the piece and the grade earned in the context of a given course, but with what is communicated to the student about that evaluation. Collecting papers at the end of the term and not returning them communicates something: that a readers' response is not an important part of the writing act. Collecting in-process papers and responding to them individually communicates something else; that revising is an expected part of the writing process. Marking all the errors on a finished manuscript communicates still another message: that surface structure errors are what writing is all about.

FIGURE 8.1

TYPICAL TEACHER COMMENTS ON STUDENT WRITING

could be kept if both partners had

journals and set aside time to compare

and examine information with

You were supposed to do that!

each other. These solutions are simple

and practical and if they were

followed more strictly the sults would

probably improve and a better

report could be made.

proof-reading!

Also, if the xperimentors took

more time to be coareful they would not

have lost as many flies as a result of

need more info on these problems

etherization, opening the jars or

counting them.

The point to be made with the

sulutions presented in this paper is that

sp

they all require more of a sacrifice

on the part of the experimentors to be

dedicated to obtaining good results

awk!

What do you recommend?

the best way they can. And all this can be

botained with more effort on the

experimentors part.

apos.

FIGURE 8.1 (continued)

TYPICAL TEACHER COMMENTS ON STUDENT WRITING

As a closing note, the results

of our experiment were considered

successful and acceptable. And, our final

ratios were approximately 9/2.8/2.8/.9

while the ideal would have been 9/3/3/1.

*your results are better than your writing.
Not enough details; too many errors!*

GOALS OF RESPONDING TO STUDENT WRITING

If asked, most teachers would have a ready answer to questions about the purposes of grading student papers. The goals are to reward good work and to offer criticism. The threat or promise of a grade is supposed to motivate students. Each of these goals is, of course, worthwhile. Yet external motivation for doing good work may be incompatible with the cultivation of efficient and satisfying writing habits. As with all other aspects of the art of teaching, goals and methods should be synchronized when it comes to evaluating writing.

Assigning grades is only one way of responding to student writing, albeit a very necessary way in our system of education. Other aspects of response have to do with how the papers are used in class, how mistakes and misunderstandings are pointed out and worked on, how teachers use their own experience with the writing process. Each earlier chapter of this book includes some suggestions for responding to and evaluating student writing in ways which will encourage openness and experimentation, yet give students direction in refining and controlling what they write. In general these suggestions have emphasized the following considerations:

1. Not all writing should receive a grade; regular, informal writing without the pressure of evaluation should be a regular part of all coursework.

2. Other class activities, such as the encouragement of questions and discussion, help establish a constructive attitude toward writing.
3. A description of how a piece of writing will be evaluated should be included in the directions for every writing assignment.
4. Complex writing tasks should be supervised during early stages of writing rather than merely graded after they are finished.
5. Teachers have many more options in responding to student writing than they take advantage of regularly.

Thus it seems evident that grading is not merely a matter of upholding standards (i.e., of giving low grades) or grading easy. The grade assigned, in fact, may not have nearly so much to do with what students learn about writing as how the writing is introduced and otherwise used in the classwork.

All of the above suggests that traditional grading against an absolute or relative standard is but one option among many in responding to student papers. Earlier chapters explain more fully other ways of helping students know the effects of what they have written. From how the writing is used the writer gets a notion of the function of writing rather than a judgment about his or her ability.

In short, there are many potential purposes for responding to student writing, only one of which is to judge it. Some of these other purposes are listed in Figure 8.2. Although each of these goals is worthy, it is not possible to attend to all of them in any one assignment, and they are not equally appropriate for all writing tasks. Informal writing offers the perfect form for dialogue and appreciation for variety; it is ruined as an opportunity for risk-taking when critical judgments intervene. On the other hand, a response to a rough

---

FIGURE 8.2

GOALS OF RESPONSES TO STUDENT WRITING

1. Judging it against relative or absolute standards.
2. Establishing a more private dialogue than can be accomplished in class discussions.
3. Improving students' attitude toward the joys and uses of writing.
4. Modeling appreciation for variety and differences among individuals.
5. Building students' self-confidence.
6. Encouraging critical thinking, insights.
7. Offering strategies and information that will lead to improvement in writing ability.
8. Promoting an interest in the methods and content of a particular discipline.
9. Inspiring risk-taking.
10. Developing in students a sense of readers' needs, a lessening of egocentricity.
11. Requiring effort, discipline, and efficiency.
12. Communicating a sense of the teacher's proficiency and concern.

FIGURE 8.3

APPROPRIATE RESPONSES FOR DIFFERENT KINDS OF WRITING

	Informal Writing	*In-process Drafts*	*Finished Manuscripts*
Examples	Journals In-class responses Letters and notes	Research papers Artistic pieces (Some essay tests)	Research papers Project reports Examinations
Appropriate goals (from Figure 8.2)	2, 3, 4, 5, 6, 8, 9, 10	3, 5, 6, 7, 8, 10, 11, 12	1, 11, 12
Options	Reading in class Response of peers in small groups Written questions Written comments	Duplicating for class to read Response of peers in small groups Written questions Revision and edit- ing worksheets Conferences	Reporting to class Grades End comments Evaluation checklists Spot checks

draft is a more appropriate place to introduce readers' needs than is the final marking of a typed and edited manuscript. Figure 8.3 outlines a sampling of different kinds of writing assignments with the goals and response options most appropriate to them.

It should be obvious that the goals that can be accomplished in response to finished manuscripts are very limited in comparison to the goals that can be accomplished in response to informal writing or in-process drafts. Responses to informal writing should be non-judgmental and supportive while coaxing forth further elaboration. Errors in informal writing should never be marked as this detracts from focus on ideas and openness. Responses to in-process drafts should focus on the strengths and weaknesses of the writing with a view to making changes that will enhance effectiveness according to the intended purpose and audience. Responses to content and organization should precede reactions to style and mechanics. Finally, responses to finished manuscripts need not be detailed unless further revision is necessary. Otherwise all that is needed is a helpful interpretation of the grade. In other words, most of the opportunities for writing instruction occur prior to the submission of a finished manuscript. The other important implication, however, is that responses to finished manuscripts need not take as much time as we are wont to give them.

JUDGE OR COACH

In responding to student writing the teacher chooses between two roles: that of judge or that of coach. As judge the teacher is using his or her vast experience with the written code and his or her role as arbiter in the classroom to hand down a verdict to the student. English teachers have too long played this role, and there is no reason for content teachers to imitate it. In fact, content teachers have the advantage of being able to shift the judging role back to the English departments while they assume the much more attractive role of coach.

As a writing coach, the content teacher can encourage students for "the big game," meaning the test, the research report, or the writing that will be required later in the students' careers. The content teacher also can share the strategies they use in writing, especially notetaking and questioning techniques. By their insistence on quantity they can reinforce the idea of exercise, making writing an ongoing part of the educational process and not just a talent to be saved up for certain show-off occasions. By their openness to different kinds of writing, they can encourage a healthier attitude toward the innate satisfactions of the writing process. By the way they respond to student writing they can build students' confidence about their own abilities. In short, the more a content teacher models good writing attitudes, the more valid writing will seem to students.

DECISION POINTS IN RESPONDING TO STUDENT WRITING

Some idea of the way an assignment will be evaluated figures into the design of the project from the first. Teachers must be sure of how the assignment fits in with other parts of a course, and they must be aware of their assumptions and options in this regard. Their decision points, at a minimum, must consider the following questions:

1. Given the skills of the students and goals of the course, what are the most important aspects of this assignment to respond to?
2. Will students learn more from a detailed critique or a short comment at the end of the paper?
3. Is teacher-time best spent offering suggestions at the early stages of writing or editing the finished manuscript?
4. How should I recognize what is said rather than seem preoccupied with *how* it is said?
5. Will revisions be allowed?
6. Do I prefer to play the role of coach or of judge?

In making these decisions the content teacher has an advantage over the English teacher on grading: end-of-term grades can be based on mastery of content as revealed on tests or in the performance of some task, not on writing ability per se. Some writing, such as the keeping of journals, can be viewed as preparation for graded activities rather than as something which has to be graded itself. Yet students must be given credit for completing writing tasks, and all writing tasks must be responded to in some way.

CONTENT VERSUS MECHANICS

Many teachers ask how much to grade content and how much to grade mechanics. At the heart of this question is the notion that spelling and punctuation can somehow be isolated from the information conveyed; also that mechanics should be taught in English class rather than "counted against" students of history or science.

It is one of the tenets of school-wide writing programs, however, that form and content are inseparable. One grade should reflect the whole production, although there may be a requirement to edit errors before the paper is credited at all.

The problem comes in expecting legislation (in the form of announcing the expectation of accurate spelling and punctuation) to overcome the inexperience of some student writers. Many simply lack the background in reading and the practice with writing to assure them of control. Fear of writing and poor instruction are additional causes of inaccuracies and contortions, often resulting in hypercorrection (apostrophes in simple plurals, for instance).

The fact is that no amount of direct instruction in grammar and drill can compensate for actual experience with the written word —both reading it and producing it! Thus improvement in mechanical accuracy is much more likely to result from systematic practice, with selective instruction in context, than in wholesale marking of all errors observed in a given piece of writing.

Conversely, it is wrong to ignore spelling and punctuation mistakes altogether on the grounds that those are problems for an English class. The truth is that deviations from standard usage detract from any piece of writing and hence become a part of the message conveyed. Insistence on care during the editing process is just as important in any other discipline as it is in English. In fact, the lessons taught in English class have significance only if they are reinforced elsewhere. How to set realistic expectations on mechanics and how to deal with errors will be more fully discussed in the suggestions below.

UNDERSTANDING THE DEVELOPMENTAL PROCESS

Although whole books have been written about how writing is learned, most classroom teachers have neither the time nor the inclination to study them. Nor should they be expected to understand the intricacies of language and learning, given that their expertise lies well outside of this specialization. Still, as teachers respond to students' writing, they reveal their attitudes and experience with language. It is best if those responses reflect what is now known about developmental learning processes.

As has already been stated, the problem of responding to errors is of primary importance in evaluating student writing. It is here that some knowledge of recent research is particularly useful. Figure 8.4 is a distillation of research findings converted into guidelines for the establishment of a policy on handling mechanical errors. Each of the guidelines implies certain other ramifications. For example, if language is always changing, it may be inadvisable to insist on the passive voice in lab reports as "the right way," although it may very well be insisted upon as a preference. Another implication is that insisting on formal prose before students have had enough experience reading it often results in bizarre parodies of what it should be.

REALISTIC EXPECTATIONS

Careful assessment of writing skills, thoughtful design of writing tasks, and early intervention in the writing process will help prevent disappointments at evaluation time. Even so, it is advisable to have some strategies for dealing with mechanical errors. The strategies should mandate quality without equating that term with mechanical accuracy alone.

Teachers might establish a set of priorities for corrections based on such principles as:

1. Do not assume that "simple" word mix-ups (*too* for *to*, *their* for *there*, etc.) or sentence structure problems (writing fragments, for instance) are simple to correct.
2. Mark first those errors which are easily corrected.
3. Mark errors which affect meaning rather than display "politeness."
4. Mark errors which exhibit regularities in the language rather than exceptions—and generalize these.
5. Mark errors which affect understanding of the discipline (including specialized uses of vocabulary) rather than niceties of usage.

Following the above principles and modifying them to suit the observed skill levels of particular students, a teacher might point out to students only the following errors in a social studies paper:

1. Spelling likely to be re-used and easily fit into patterns, but not all misspelled words. For example, mark *goverment* and *envirement*, but not *basicly* or *Kennedies*.
2. Commas around extra words, but not commas mistakenly inserted between two sentences where a period was required. For example, mark "The funeral of President Kennedy, for example was a very public affair." Do not mark "President Johnson was sworn in, it happened on the presidential airplane."
3. Commonly used verb forms that reveal dialectical differences, but not "literary" verb forms such as the subjunctive voice. For example, mark "he seen" or "he done," but not "If it was true."
4. Mix-ups over specialized vocabulary, but not refinements of word usage. For example, mark misunderstandings of minority *whip* and *branch* of government, but not usages such as *legislature* as an adjective (instead of *legislative*) or *judge* instead of *judicial*.

By using restraint in the marking of errors and by calling attention only to those problems which are easy to correct and which affect understanding of the content, teachers are showing concern for the developmental process rather than expecting ideal performance prematurely. After sensitive observation of student performance in writing and student responses to previous corrections, teachers develop a sense of what to stress in their responses to student writing.

RESPONDING EARLY IN THE WRITING PROCESS

An ideal time for careful correcting of errors is after the first-draft. Very often students can help each other at this stage. Every class has several students who can spell well and who are more fully aware of writing conventions than others. These students could serve as editors for their peers, not only spotting mistakes, but also identifying unclear explanations and suggesting where more support is needed. When point systems or checklists are used, even relatively unsophisticated students can serve as respondents of each other's early work, offering suggestions for revision and editing.

Most of the evaluation methods discussed below are appropriate for responses early in the writing process rather than evaluation of the finished process. The fact is that early intervention is much more effective pedagogically.

FIGURE 8.4

GUIDELINES FOR RESPONDING TO STUDENT ERRORS

1. Acceptable language usage is always in a state of gradual change although the conventions of writing are generally more conservative than what is considered acceptable in speaking.

   e.g., *Who* is gradually becoming acceptable instead of *whom* in such sentences as "It was Tom who I saw."

2. All errors are not equally serious.

   e.g., Misspelling an irregular word like "separate" is not nearly so serious as misspelling a regular one like "writing."

3. Print awareness must precede ability to revise and edit.

   e.g., A word repeatedly misspelled will not necessarily reinforce that misspelling (except kinesthetically) because the writer is not consciously considering the spelling.

4. Writing is sufficiently complex that writers must perform many operations automatically rather than deliberately.

   e.g., A student still paying primary attention to such lower order matters as spelling can't focus on the higher order considerations, such as control of tone.

5. People learn first those features of language which carry meaning. If they are directly taught features which they have not experienced in reading, they will make errors of "hyper-correction." This is especially true of punctuation.

   e.g., The six piston's were working.

6. In learning new words or sentence structures, students often pass through a period of misuse before the new form seems natural. This is especially true for forms associated with formal prose, but not characteristic of everyday talk.

   e.g., That was the experiment in which was successful.

7. Students will write more accurately and fluently if the topic engages their interest.

   e.g., Convoluted sentences on essay tests may result from anxiety and insecurity about the information rather than because of lack of skill per se.

PEER EVALUATION

When teachers are willing to relinquish some of their control over evaluation and students have been properly prepared, peer groups can take partial responsibility for evaluation that leads to revision.

Peer evaluation has several advantages. First, it takes some of the load off the teacher. Secondly, it serves as a powerful motivator to underachieving students. When control is turned over to the students, they tend to claim "ownership" for what they write (rather than refer to "what the teacher wants"); they tend to observe more about what they and their classmates write; and they develop a mature understanding of the reasons for taking care while writing: that readers' needs must be met.

Earlier chapters (especially Chapter 2) describe ways to encourage students to work collaboratively in small groups, responding to each other's informal writing as well as using notes for other class tasks. The capstone of these small group activities can come from the help trained students can give each other in revising and editing their more complicated writing assignments.

Students can serve this function by listening to each other's rough drafts, editing each other's papers just before the final manuscript is copied, or proofreading the final manuscript just before it is turned in. For rough drafts students might each read their papers aloud to their groups, with group members responding to these kinds of questions:

- What parts of the paper are especially effective and why?
- What would you like to hear more about?
- What questions about the topic do you as a reader still have?

Answers to these questions can be given to the writer orally and written down in brief form by the writer of the paper for later reference. Or each student can write answers down and give them to the writer. In these ways the writer comes to learn what has been communicated to readers and what needs further work. Since the paper is still in-process, there is no need to suggest editing corrections. At later stages of the process peers can offer suggestions for rearrangement or editing. Checklists are especially effective for revising and editing (see examples below).

Although the satisfactions of peer evaluations are innate, some students may need monitoring until they are used to assuming this responsibility for themselves. Monitoring can take the form of recording behaviors as students work together or collecting checklists before they are given to the student writers. As the usefulness of peer evaluation becomes evident, however, student participation will require less and less structure.

Lest content teachers worry about the "time taken away" from content material when classes are devoted to peer evaluation, they should be reminded that time spent in this way is really "on task." Students engaged in discussing their papers are engaged in discussing the subject matter at hand; very often new information about the subject is learned. Misunderstandings are also cleared up. Best of all, students thus engaged become active learners and take responsibility for their own work.

FIGURE 8.5

POINT SYSTEM FOR A RESEARCH PAPER IN MATH CLASS

10 points for each "yes," 0 points for each "no."

	yes	no
1. Rough draft done on due date for in-class revision groups?	____	____
*2. Paper begins with a quotation adequately introduced and documented?	____	____
*3. Separate parts of the quotation rephrased in student's own words?	____	____
4. Evidence of a thorough understanding of the topic and well explained?	____	____
5. Good transitions between different parts of the paper?	____	____
*6. Inclusion of the connection between the topic and material in the textbook?	____	____
*7. Inclusion of some application of the topic to a real-life situation?	____	____
8. Length at least ten fully developed paragraphs?	____	____
9. Spelling of words from math vocabulary list accurate?	____	____
*10. List of sources, including publishers and dates, included?	____	____

"yes" TOTAL   ____ (100
possible)
$\times$ 10 =   ____

(90–100 = A; 80–89 = B; 70–79 = C; 60–69 = D)

TOTAL POINT SYSTEM FOR THIS MATH CLASS:

homework	100
quizzes	200
exam	100
paper	100
per term	500

*These items were peculiar to the particular assignment and specified in the directions.

POINT SYSTEMS

If absolute judgment of quality is inappropriate, teachers can adopt a point system which gives students credit for quantity or fulfillment of other specifications rather than quality per se. One system for doing this is simply to award points for completion of assignments. This is a particularly effective way to count reaction papers, journal entries, and expressive writing because it eliminates the need for identifying and correcting mistakes. In some cases the writing need not even be read by the teacher, especially if it is to serve as the basis of small group work, since students will learn from their peers if their writings are acceptable or not.

The advantages of grading on quantity rather than quality are many. Pieces of writing are evaluated more quickly and many of the bad feelings about writing are eliminated. As has already been mentioned, nothing is more discouraging to a student than to work hard on a piece of writing which receives a bad grade. Nothing is more discouraging for a teacher than having to correct errors or having to explain why low grades were assigned. When graded for completing a writing task, students need not worry specifically about their grades. Yet they still gain valuable practice with writing and come to experience its innate satisfactions. Writing becomes appreciated as a means of controlling data and making connections rather than always serving as a vehicle for displaying what the student already knows.

Point systems can also be used to objectify qualitative grades, to regularize or complement the editing marks and comments on a paper. Thus point systems can also be adapted to more formal writing assignments that serve as measures of understanding rather than means of learning the information. In other words, research papers, reports, and essays can be graded on quantitative scales rather than according to absolute standards or ideal performances. Students are awarded points for adherence to certain specified and measurable traits in the assignment, including length. These traits might include kinds of illustrations, distinctly labeled sub-headings, or the number of sources consulted. Figure 8.5 outlines a point system for a research paper done for math class and based on interviews. By making each trait a matter of "acceptable" or "unacceptable" (by means of a "forced choice" response), the teacher using this kind of a checklist has a very easy job of responding to a batch of student papers. Students receiving such a checklist in response to what they write know exactly why they've received the grade they did. Or, if the evaluation was done early in the writing process, students know what they need to revise if the paper is to be acceptable.

In setting up a point system teachers should determine an appropriate maximum proportion of the total to assign to each trait measured. Usually the number of points which make the difference between two contiguous grades is appropriate, so that a student can raise or lower the grade by one letter through conscientious writing effort. If other components of the course, such as test scores or class participation, are to be included in the point system, then attention must be given to the proportion of work involved in the writing assignment relative to the other parts of the coursework. Figure 8.6 represents one teacher's explanation of a point system for one term of chemistry.

The lab reports expected in this chemistry class were easy to evaluate because of the clearly delineated point system. One important aspect of that point system was the way length was described as a matter of paragraphing rather than as a matter of word counts. Nothing is more discouraging for student writers than to count numbers of words as a measure of whether they've completed an assignment adequately. The point system outlined in Figure 8.6 also reinforces the importance of the writing by counting the writing heavily in comparison to scores on class tests.

CHECKLISTS

Even without the assignment of points, checklists of various sorts are useful in responding to early drafts and in grading finished papers. Checklists can be individualized to suit the criteria of a specific paper. They also save the teacher time by listing the criteria of evaluation, so each paper does not have to be individually explained. Figure 8.7 represents a checklist appropriate for a particular writing assignment from a psychology class:

> Define motivation, using sources and class activities which seem relevant. Support your definition with explanation and illustrations.

The checklist was devised after the teacher compared a successful composition with an unsuccessful one to determine significant traits.

One advantage of using a "Primary Trait Checklist" is that the different traits of a given paper can be counted according to their relative importance. In weighing the various traits for the psychology paper, for example, this teacher decided that following directions should receive more weight than editing skills or understanding the rhetorical context. Another feature of the checklist shown in Figure 8.7 is the minimal attention it diverts to mechanical accuracy. By relegating that consideration to a simple count, the teacher is saved from total preoccupation with errors while yet paying mechanical accuracy enough attention that a good grade cannot be earned with-

FIGURE 8.6
_____

POINT SYSTEM EXPECTED OF CHEMISTRY STUDENTS*

Trait to be evaluated	Points possible	Points awarded
1. Format according to directions, sections clearly labeled, spaced, in prescribed order.	5	_____
2. Purpose statement written in own words with verb from purpose list.	5	_____
3. List of equipment correctly spelled.	5	_____
4. Procedures listed by steps, but stated in the third person, past tense, not as directions.	10	_____
5. Results summarized with separate paragraph for each distinct operation, making sure something from each step of procedure and reference to each "total" on data sheet included.	15	_____
6. Conclusions distinct from results and general principles revealed with applications or suggestions for future experimenters.	10	_____
TOTAL AWARDED OUT OF	50	= _____

Point System for Term of Chemistry:
lab reports @ 50 ea.   = 150
journal @ 1 pt. per page to a maximum = 50
tests @ 50 ea.   = 100
                                              _____
per term   300

(270–300 = A; 240–269 = B; 210–239 = C; 180–209 = D)

*Could be adapted for other subjects.

_____

out it. Again, an error count of six per page was chosen arbitrarily as a rough approximation of Shaughnessy's reader toleration level.[5] That number could be adjusted for different ability levels and age levels, depending on whether any class time had been devoted to editing or not. Primary trait checklists are adaptable to any type of writing assignment, including essay test answers. (See other samples in Chapter 5.)

   Many "commercial" or general checklists are usable without adaptation for any writing assignment. Typically these list such items as organization, sentence structure, and mechanics. The limitation

FIGURE 8.7
___

PRIMARY TRAIT SCORE SHEET FOR A PSYCHOLOGY PAPER*

DIRECTIONS:
Listed below are the traits considered important for this assignment. These traits were listed on the original directions for the assignment. Each trait has been converted into a description that would earn points, 0 being a poor job on that trait and the higher numbers representing a good job. The most valued trait (in this case, following directions) earns the most points. Only one number is circled under each trait.

Points   Traits

Following Directions:
0   does not define motivation.

1   defines motivation, but explanation does not include other concepts from the textbook or class notes.

2   defines motivation and includes other concepts from the textbook or class notes, but explanation is unsupported or support is unexplained.

3   defines motivation, includes other concepts, explains these, and uses adequate support.

Intellectual Strategies:
0   sticks to a series of literal-level recalls, or combines information illogically.

1   combines information to reach a logical insight.

2   maintains consistency in mustering evidence to support that insight.

Development:
0   offers no interplay between generalizations and examples.

1   alternates generalizations with examples, but with inadequate attention to explaining the connections.

2   presents generalizations, explains them, and offers relevant examples.

Organization:
0   lacks traditional paragraphing or seems unorganized.

1   has thesis and regular paragraphs, but lacks cohesion.

2   contains logical groupings with clear transitions so that an outline could easily be made from what is written.

Understanding the Rhetorical Context:
0   assumes an inappropriate tone (too informal or pseudo-scholarly).

1   assumes an appropriate tone for most of the paper or all of the paper.

Mechanics:
0   averages six or more discrete errors in spelling, punctuation, or sentence structure per page.

1   averages fewer than six discrete errors in spelling, punctuation, or sentence structure per page, but handwriting does not present a neat appearance.

FIGURE 8.7 (continued)

PRIMARY TRAIT SCORE SHEET FOR A PSYCHOLOGY PAPER*

2   contains few errors in spelling, punctuation, or sentence structure and presents neat, clear manuscript form.

TOTAL POINTS OUT OF 12 _____

*Could be adapted for other topics.

FIGURE 8.8

GENERALIZED CHECKLIST

Checkmarks indicate judgment of quality on each item.

	Good	Average	Poor
Content:			
1. Subject and treatment done according to directions.			
2. Organization purposeful.			
3. Development full (alternation of generalizations with specifics).			
Mechanics:			
1. Sentence structure and punctuation mature and varied.			
2. Spelling correct.			
3. Verb forms and tense standard and consistent.			
4. Pronoun references and misc. usage carefully done.			
Style:			
1. Diction and vocabulary used conventionally.			
2. Level of formality appropriate.			
3. Quotations and documentation handled according to directions.			

GENERAL COMMENTS:

OVERALL GRADE: _____

is that they almost always overemphasize form at the expense of content. Figure 8.8 represents such a general checklist. As has already been discussed, there is a danger in responding only to the formal aspects of a paper and ignoring its particular content. Individual idiosyncracies, including sometimes surprisingly mature insights, are not taken into account on generalized checklists. Therefore, any checklist should also be accompanied by an open-ended category or a place for comments on what was communicated in the writing. Otherwise students get the feeling that no one really caught their message.

HOLISTIC EVALUATION

If the only purpose of evaluating a set of papers is to sort them or to grade them, such as would be the case for a final evaluation or an entrance test, experienced teachers may choose to use holistic evaluation. By this method the evaluator is not concerned about specific traits in the writing or about particular criteria (though subconsciously the teacher may very well be working from an implicit primary trait checklist based on his or her own particular biases). Instead, the teacher reads numerous papers until he or she develops an intuitive feel for the balance of more successful and unsuccessful papers, allowing for quite different balances of individual traits. For example, originality may compensate for organizational shortcomings, or, in other cases, mature sentence structure may compensate for numerous spelling errors. The point is that holistic or "impressionistic" judgment can be subjected to more rigorous and time-consuming checks and counts. However, on final drafts or entrance tests there may be no particular need to inform the writer of the reasons for the judgment so long as the judgment itself is valid.

TRADITIONALLY GRADED PAPERS

The paper marked with editing symbols, marginal notes, and end comments can also be done effectively, but students need to know the proofreading symbols used. These can be prominently posted or learned from a handbook. Students should learn them and practice using them prior to being expected to interpret them. Figure 8.9 lists some of the more common proofreading symbols which might prove useful for editing in a content course. If editing symbols such as these are to be effective, students must be motivated to pay attention to them. Teachers can provide motivation either punitively or through support. Grading harshly when errors abound is the most common policy, the easiest to legislate, and the least effective pedagogically. Premature insistence on absolute accuracy encourages plagiarism or unacknowledged help. It may also have the effect of causing students to be overly cautious, using only simple words and structures. Better is a policy which supports risk-taking and allows students to correct errors without undue punishment.

Allowing Revisions

Some teachers grade low when errors abound and raise the grade if corrections are made. This policy, however, puts mechanical errors in the wrong perspective, making it seem that accuracy is an added bonus to writing rather than a factor which should be assumed. Furthermore, students learn to count on their teachers to find errors rather than assuming responsibility for them. The upwardly revised grades are sometimes inflated since major revisions are not usually undertaken as part of the "correcting" required.

Withholding Grades

An imaginative way of getting students to understand both editing symbols and end-comments is to offer them without a grade. After

---

FIGURE 8.9

COMMON PROOFREADING SYMBOLS

Symbol	Meaning	Symbol	Meaning
ℋ	new paragraph	ww	wrong word
ℓ	omit	ss	sentence structure
∽	transpose	sp	spelling
∧	insert	cap	capitalization
◡	make one word	agr	agreement
X	obvious error	t	tense
tr	transition needed	p	punctuation (with the particular mark noted)
//	parallel structure	ref	referent unclear

---

reading through these marks and comments (and thus assessing the seriousness of the revisions being suggested), students must choose between doing the suggested revisions *or* receiving their grade. Once the grade is revealed, however, the student forfeits the possibility of improving that grade by revising. This approach serves three purposes: it causes students to read through the comments rather than glance only at the grade; it grants them control over the decision to make the suggested corrections; and it prevents the problem of giving higher and higher grades as a motivator for continuing the revision process.

Mandating Corrections

Another method of requiring the correction of annoying surface errors without assigning artificially high grades to papers which are mechanically accurate or artificially low grades to those which are not, is to assign a grade on the basis of criteria appropriate to the assignment. Then specify which errors must absolutely be corrected if that assigned grade is to be retained. Allow a reasonable time limit for the corrections and make sure there is a realistic chance that students can make the corrections—either with tutors, at a writing lab, or on their own. After that extension period the paper automatically becomes an F. This policy emphasizes the importance of accuracy and assigns responsibility for revision where it belongs: on the student.

Written Comments

In addition to editing symbols and marginal comments, traditionally graded papers usually include some kind of end-comment. Such comments serve different purposes. For a quick review of the kinds of written comments teachers have to choose from, see Figure 8.10.

FIGURE 8.10

CLASSIFYING TEACHER RESPONSES TO PUPILS' WRITTEN WORK

Type of Teacher Response	Focus of Teacher Response	
	Content	Form
Evaluation	Good story! Excellent! Poor ideas! Your best work!	Well-written! Good word choice. Poor sentence structure.

FIGURE 8.10 (continued)

CLASSIFYING TEACHER RESPONSES TO PUPILS' WRITTEN WORK

Type of Teacher Response	Focus of Teacher Response	
	Content	Form
Assessment	I see that you know the subject.	You are beginning to use paragraphs.
Instructional a) didactic/correction	The way people treated the boy is an example of prejudice.	You have several spelling mistakes. Use indentions to signal this new idea.
b) encouragement	This was very exciting. You should write more.	You used a good variety of sentences. Keep up the good work!
c) comment on attitude	You haven't researched this very well—try harder.	Don't be so careless with your spelling and handwriting.
Audience a) clarification	I don't understand what happened here. Can you explain?	Misplaced modifier. Where is your topic sentence?
b) elaboration	What would this feel like?	Use more descriptive vocabulary.
c) reaction	I enjoyed that. I felt what you would feel if that happened. I think that should be in the class paper.	You have beautiful handwriting. I'm impressed by your vocabulary.
d) taking action	Change a classroom procedure in response to a written request.	Have a lesson on quotation marks after seeing that most students in class could not use this in their stories.
Moving outside the writing a) extension	Tell me more! Have you considered what Bill says?	This anecdote would make a good starting point for a play.
b) addition	Let me tell you what happened to me. I disagree with what you say.	Your work reminds me of the poetry of e.e. cummings.

Source: Reprinted with permission from Dennis Searle and David Dillon, "Responding to Student Writing: What Is Said or How It Is Said," Language Arts 57 (October 1980): 777.

Probably most teachers write comments on a very limited set of observations, more often focusing on form rather than content. This may be because errors are more readily recognizable in that realm. But whatever the reason, the message communicated to students is that form is more important than content. Better would be a deliberate effort on the part of teachers to respond with comments asking for clarification or elaboration. The modeling of comments that state personal reactions to content are especially unusual. One teacher found that his students continually misinterpreted his personal reaction statements, assuming he meant them as evaluation or assessment. Sometimes it is as hard for students to break out of *their* response habits as it is for teachers.

For final, finished papers on which the student had previously received suggestions for revision, the teacher's comment need only justify the grade assessment. A limited comment on the final paper requires much more self-control by the teacher, but gives the student a better sense of how he or she did.

The comment on the paper in Figure 8.11 relates the grade to the purpose of the assignment and how well it satisfied its readers' needs. Furthermore, the comment reveals a close, thoughtful reading. Besides being content-specific, the comments make this particular assignment relevant to other parts of the classwork. The comments communicate respect for the integrity of the writer: they are courteous.

TAPE RECORDINGS

Because written comments may be ignored or misinterpreted, some teachers prefer to explain their criticism orally on cassette tapes. Most students have access to cassette tape recorders and are happy to submit a blank tape with each major paper. They like getting taped responses, too, for several reasons: the tapes seem more personal, they can be listened to at home, and, in the meantime, their unmarked papers seem more respected without the molestation of marks—red or otherwise. Teachers report that the tape recordings do not take any more time than careful written comments since no time is taken for rewinding or playing back the tapes. Students report that they like the tapes because they can listen several times and what they hear seems more personal than written comments. Perhaps the novelty alone makes cassette tapes a fresh experience for both teacher and student.

CONFERENCES

Another method of giving oral instead of written responses is to talk directly with the student about his or her paper. Conferences are especially useful when papers are still in-process and there is time to revise. This conferencing need not be done outside of class; it can be scheduled "on the run" within five- or ten-minute sessions while other class members are busy on another activity. Conferences work particularly well when the teacher is familiar with the students' work, perhaps because of individualized record-keeping, such as that suggested in Chapter 3 on assessment.

Students bring their papers to the teacher's desk with specific questions to ask. Sometimes students can be asked to prepare for a conference by looking critically at their own papers, perhaps by means of a conference preparation sheet such as presented in Figure 8.12. Figure 8.12, adaptable for other tasks and subjects, is designed specifically for a book critique in physics class. By asking the student to

---

FIGURE 8.11
_____

MEANINGFUL END COMMENTS ON A STUDENT PAPER

The point to be made with the sulutions presented in this paper is that all they require more of a sacrifice on the part of the experimentors to be dedicated to obtaining good results the best way they can. And all this can be botained with more effort on the experimentors part.

As a closing note, the results of our experiment were considered successful and acceptable. And, our final ratios were approximately 9/2.8/2.8/.9 while the ideal would have been 9/3/3/1.

If future experimenters are going to avoid making the mistakes you made, they will need to know more exactly what you did wrong during etherization and counting. Lack of proofreading can make it seem you were careless in the experimenting in spite of your good results numerically.

*The paper is the same one used for Figure 8.1

---

find evidence of attention to the purpose and audience for the paper, the teacher has turned responsibility over to the student for applying what was discussed in class. Also, the specialized questions guarantee that the conference will have a limited focus. Because certain parts of the paper have already been singled out for study by the student, the teacher need not read through the whole paper.

Another style of conference might have the teacher glance quickly over the paper and suggest two or three things yet to be worked on. Rather than give directives for changes in this conference, it is better if the teacher poses questions and has the student come up with alternatives, again so that the student assumes responsibility for decisions. Here are the kinds of questions that might lead to the generation of alternatives, the sense of choice:

- What one sentence sums up your main point? (This question leads to other questions about what is unclear about the main point, what might be a better way to state the main point, where is the main point contradicted in the paper, etc.)
- What is the connection between this part of your paper and this part? (This question leads to other questions about the over-all organization of the paper, the needs of the readers for full explanation, the ways to achieve transitions, etc.)

FIGURE 8.12

CONFERENCE PREPARATION SHEET FOR PHYSICS

Before you come up for your conference, mark the following things lightly in pencil on your paper:

1. The sentence which best sums up your main point about the book.

2. Examples of three kinds of transition between sections of your report.

3. A place where you introduced a quotation and commented on it.

4. An idea which appears as a generalization, is explained, then illustrated.

5. A place that seems awkward or unclear to you.

In addition, be able to answer the following questions, if asked:

1. What are the strengths and weaknesses of your paper?

2. What ideas about the book were you conscious of leaving out of your report? Why did you?

3. What kind of help would you like on this paper?

Source: Based on an assignment reviewing Thomas Kuhn's *The Structure of Scientific Revolutions* (Chicago: University of Chicago Press, 1975).

- Listen closely as I read this part to you and tell me how someone unfamiliar with the topic might react. (This question leads to questions about readers' assumptions, level of formality or conventions of writing, and the need for fuller explanation.)

The advantage of conferences is that the teacher need not spend out-of-class time reading the papers. Also, the students listen better one-on-one than they do in generalized class sessions, even when many students share the same writing problems. The disadvantage of conferencing is that students may keep no record of what was explained unless they write things down themselves (which is a good policy). Record-keeping can be a problem. Also, conferencing won't work in extremely large classes or lecture-oriented classes. It works well when independent work and small groups are encouraged. Since many teachers use conferences as an "after-the-fact" chance to justify an assigned grade or as a forum for debate with students over grades, it may take a while for some students to accept conferences for constructive or collaborative work on unfinished papers. A hidden benefit, however, is the simple result that pre-writing and incubation are encouraged by the scheduling of conferences. Regular conferences can eliminate last minute writing efforts as the cause of poorly done papers.

LETTERS

Since writing is such an act of commitment, with the writer's personality being on the line, great care should be taken in commenting on and criticizing the written product. It is not that comments need be unrealistically positive, but that tones of moral condemnation should be avoided. Sometimes it helps to think of each writer as a potentially important adult at a very troubled time of life, especially since that is very likely to be the case. One way to achieve this respectful tone is to frame comments in a letter, using the student's name and signing it with your own. Figure 8.13 represents such an effort. A letter, such as the one in Figure 8.13, could stand alone, or a shorter version of it could be appended to a standardized checklist in place of regular end-comments. Form letters explaining criteria and justifying assigned grades could also be enclosed as responses to finished papers.

PROCESS SPOT CHECKS

Teachers who are concerned that students follow the correct process in writing complicated papers can save themselves time in evaluating

FIGURE 8.13

LETTER RESPONSE TO STUDENT PAPER

Dear Jim,

    Your critique of Kuhn's book made interesting reading for the intended audience because you explained all the scientific terms well. Your selection of the quotation about regular science was a good choice for analysis. If your proof-reading had been as thorough as your analysis, you would have earned an A instead of a B. Keep up the good work!

               Sincerely,

               Mr. Stratman

---

that aspect of the task by initiating a process spot check. Students are directed to bring their raw data (note cards, logs, interview records, etc.), their rough drafts, and their finished manuscripts to class on the due date. Then they are directed to select three different pieces of recorded data to follow through on their rough drafts and in the final manuscript. First, they circle and number three pieces of raw data. Next, they find their references to this data in their rough drafts and in their final paper, circling these references and marking each with the same number used to mark the raw data originally circled. Students may also wish to add an explanation of the changes they noted in the various versions of the material.

    In this way the teacher has a record of representative samples of transformed and revised data without having to go through the notes and revisions to dig them out. The process check also can serve as one measure of success on that paper. If students were unable to discover a progression of transformations of raw data through to the final manuscript, the teacher may wish to postpone evaluation of the paper until proof can be established that the information in the paper was indeed written by the student who claimed it and that the information was indeed modified in subsequent drafts. Thus the process check serves as a foil to plagiarism and as an assurance that the information was interpreted and integrated rather than merely absorbed piecemeal in the final manuscript—in other words, that the student actually capitalized on the writing process.

PORTFOLIOS

Yet another method of encouraging adequate revision and giving students some control in the evaluation process is to encourage portfolios or writing folders to be graded as a whole. Portfolios are useful in classes where large amounts of writing are done. Rather than grade incoming papers separately as they are turned in, each is responded to, often in peer groups. Credit may be given for completing papers on time, but students are directed to select a limited number of manuscripts for submission in a manila folder or notebook at the end of the term. These submitted manuscripts are then graded as a whole, an arrangement which allows the strengths of one paper to compensate for the weaknesses of another and vice versa, thus minimizing the disappointments students often feel when something that they have worked hard over and think well of is not given a grade as high as something they don't think as well of.

In addition to allowing the evaluator to make a quicker job of grading (since there is no necessity for extensive marking), portfolios have the additional value of resembling the way writing is evaluated in the "real world." Authors and business people submit only their best, revised work for close scrutiny by a critical reader. And they usually do not expect detailed critiques of what they submit.

THE PAYOFFS OF GOOD EVALUATION

The main point of all this discussion is that teachers should be fully aware of their options in evaluating student writing. There is a distinct relationship between their choices of options and their philosophy of learning. The approaches to evaluation discussed in this and previous chapters are meant to be suggestive rather than definitive. Each can be adapted to any discipline and each could suggest still other creative approaches to evaluation.

Good evaluation obviously rewards effective effort, provides helpful advice, and assures purposeful judgment. Beyond that, if it is suited to the task at hand, good evaluation promotes a healthy attitude toward writing by encouraging thoughtful elaboration in the early stages, offering specific suggestions for revision of early drafts, and judging the effectiveness of final manuscripts. Good evaluation not only guides the student in the writing of papers, but minimizes the drudgery of the teacher in grading papers. Obviously the kind of response a paper receives affects the way it is written in the first place. For all of these reasons evaluation of student writing cannot be an afterthought in the course which incorporates writing.

Good evaluation of student writing suits the goals for the assignment. If the goal is offering guidance for revision, then early intervention is preferable to end-of-the-term grading. If the goal is encouraging students to be self-critical, then peer-critiquing is appropriate. If the goal is measurement against established criteria, then checklists are appropriate. Rewarding work well done and offering advice for future writing projects, although obvious goals for any writing task, are simply not explicit enough to suggest one particular approach to evaluation over another.

In general, evaluation is effective when it is attended to by the student and affirmed by the student. Traditional markings and letter grades do not always achieve these ends. Better are conscious attempts to select the most significant aspects of an assignment for comment and to report these in ways that catch the students' attention and communicate respect. Students will not dread receiving evaluation and teachers will not dread giving it when the criteria are clarified from the beginning and when the mechanism is demonstrated to be both fair and appropriate.

Good evaluation not only breeds better papers in successive rounds, but also better attitudes toward writing.

NOTES

1. See, for example, discussion in Sara Freedman, "Why Teachers Give the Grades They Do," *College Composition and Communication* 30 (May 1979): 161–164.

2. John Daly and James C. McCroskey, "Occupational Desirability and Choice as a Function of Communication Apprehension," *Journal of Counseling Psychology* 22 (July 1975): 309–313.

3. Freedman, Pp. 161–162.

4. See, for example, the discussion in Robert Stiff, "The Effect Upon Student Compositions of Particular Correction Techniques," *Research in the Teaching of English* 1 (Spring 1967): 54–75.

5. Mina Shaughnessy, *Errors and Expectations* (New York: Oxford University Press, 1977), 122. Shaughnessy estimates that readers only tolerate five or six obvious errors per 300 words of writing.

9

Establishing a School-Wide Writing Program

In the age of accountability many school districts have necessarily become concerned that their graduates neither read nor write as well as they should. Many school districts and several states have even adopted minimum competency requirements in reading and writing, assuming not only that language skills can be measured objectively through standardized testing, but also hoping that the threat of testing requirements will somehow motivate mastery of the requisite skills. Many school-wide writing programs, in fact, are either motivated by testing or evaluated on the basis of it.

Actually an emphasis on testing sets up a whole series of developments which can be counterproductive to the encouragement of more and better writing. First, since standardized tests measure discrete sub-skills thought to be indicative of overall skill, they focus attention on small parts of the total writing task, parts which are often either misconstrued or misapplied out of context. Standardized tests sometimes cause English teachers to teach directly for the test. Secondly, they focus on editing rather than on composing. And third, they seem completely irrelevant to the kinds of learning done for courses other than English. With testing as the main emphasis in a school-wide writing program, it becomes very hard to involve faculty across the curriculum. Most find it easy to ignore admonitions that "writing is everybody's business" on the grounds that history or math or chemistry should then be everybody's business.

It is not difficult to see why many in-service programs to encourage writing fail. Unacknowledged resentment may contribute to a lack of receptivity to learning about writing during in-service programs. Many teachers, having sat reluctantly through years of such programs, resent the implication that they are not already doing as much as they can in the classroom, that they need to be "caught up" in their field.

Indeed, in-service programs about writing done around a lecture format—or even ones which encourage group participation (without adequate theory or an experiential component)—are doomed to failure. A destructive tendency at faculty meetings or in-service programs often accompanies discussion of writing: people just start arguing about terminology, standards, or the importance of particular errors. As mentioned in Chapter 1, most people have very personal and very definite ideas about the teaching of writing. It seems to be a surprisingly volatile issue. In fact, a whole literature has developed around ways of facilitating constructive discussion among teachers about writing.[1]

More effective are programs modeled on the Bay Area Writing Projects. Here the emphasis is on doing writing and having teachers teach each other what works well for them. Any school-wide program should seek out consultants who have had experience with seminars of the sort run by the National Area Writing Projects, now available regionally across the United States.[2] Better than single days of exposure to this approach, however, are the more extended summer sessions which inspire them.

In fact, many school-wide programs have been inspired by one or two teachers who have attended such seminars. There is something about the sharing of ideas, even the swapping of student papers that makes the extra work worth the effort when more than one teacher in a given location gets enthusiastic about incorporating more writing in content courses. Their enthusiasm, picked up in the lounge or over lunch, often inspires more inquiry into the use of writing across the curriculum.

In addition to grassroots enthusiasm, a meaningful school-wide program must have administrative support. Superintendents, principals, and department chairs must be so convinced of the benefits accruing from school-wide writing that they are willing to support them by sending teams of teachers to regional writing seminars and rewarding innovators with promotions, pay raises, or reduced course loads. Schools and systems which adopt school-wide programs also need financial support for the publications which inevitably grow out of such endeavors.

For teachers interested in stimulating interest among their colleagues about using writing in the classroom, the following steps might be useful:

1. *Take an initial survey* of all faculty members about the amount of

writing they now require, the importance they attach to writing, and the interest they have in finding out more about writing.[3]

2. *Form a committee* with representatives from various departments to read relevant literature about writing, to set policy, to select materials (including a readily available bookshelf of such resources as are listed in the bibliography of this book), and to write proposals. It is important that this committee include influential school leaders if it is to be effective.[4] Eventually such a committee might legislate a philosophy, a handbook with common terminology for reference in all classes, even an in-house publication describing the kinds of writing appropriate for different courses.

3. *Establish a network of support* for teachers using writing. This might entail regular meetings; it should definitely include newsletters and some provision for the publication of writing done in classes. An active network can reach out to similar clusters of teachers elsewhere or to regional or national conferences of professional organizations, especially of non-English subject areas.

Interestingly, in almost all schools leadership for writing across the curriculum is taken by the non-English faculty. Quite frequently the English faculty is committed instead to a more literary approach to writing or to the teaching of literature itself. The best advocates of writing across the curriculum are those who have witnessed the value of frequent and varied writing projects in their content courses and who, inspired by this, have taken to scribbling and dabbling with writing themselves. What seems obvious is that the best way to learn writing and to learn by writing is to write!

NOTES

1. For example, Randy Freisinger, "Cross Disciplinary Writing Workshops: Theory and Practice," *College English* 42 (October 1980): 154–166.

2. For a list of sites where National Writing Projects are offered, write to James Gray, Director, National Writing Project, School of Education, 5635 Tolman Hall, University of California, Berkeley, California 94720.

3. One such survey form appears in Dan Donlan, "Teaching Writing in the Content Areas: Eleven Hypotheses from a Teacher Survey," *Research in the Teaching of English* 8 (Spring 1974): 250–262.

4. For this and other ways to initiate change in educational settings, see Ronald G. Havelock, *The Change Agent's Guide to Innovation in Education* (Englewood Cliffs, New Jersey: Educational Technology Publications, 1973).

Bibliography

RESEARCH AND THEORY

Bizzell, Patricia. "Thomas Kuhn, Scientism, and the English Studies." *College English* 40 (March 1979): 764–771.

*Bloom, Benjamin, Ed. *Taxonomy of Educational Objectives: Handbook I, Cognitive Domain*. New York: David McKay Co., 1956.

Braddock, Richard, Richard Lloyd-Jones, and Lowell Schoer. *Research in Written Composition*. Urbana, Illinois: National Council of Teachers of English, 1963.

Brady, Philip L., Ed. *The "Why's" of Teaching Composition*. Urbana, Illinois: National Council of Teachers of English, 1978.

Clegg, A.B., Ed. *The Excitement of Writing*. New York: Schocken Books, 1972.

Cooper, Charles R., and Lee Odell. *Research on Composing*. Urbana, Illinois: National Council of Teachers of English, 1978.

Crooke, Edith. "Two Views of Teaching Writing." *Midwest Messenger* (February 1980): 3–12.

Daly, John, and James C. McCroskey. "Occupational Desirability and Choice as a Function of Communication Apprehension." *Journal of Counseling Psychology* 22 (July 1975): 309–313.

Daly, John. "Writing Apprehension in the Classroom: Teacher Role Expectations of the Apprehensive Writer." *Research in the Teaching of English* 13 (February 1979): 37–44.

DeFord, Diane, Ed. *Theory Into Practice*. Columbus, Ohio: Ohio State University, 1980.

*Dewey, John. *Experience and Education*. New York: Collier, 1963.

Dixon, John. *Growth Through English*. Urbana, Illinois: National Council of Teachers of English, 1975.

*Denotes works with implications for writing instruction, but little direct discussion of writing.

Donovan, Timothy, and Ben W. McClelland, Eds. *Eight Approaches to Teaching Composition.* Urbana, Illinois: National Council of Teachers of English, 1980.

Frederiksen, C., M. Whiteman, and J. Dominic, Eds. *Writing: The Nature, Development and Teaching of Written Communication.* Hillsdale, New Jersey: Erlbaum, 1980.

Garrison, Roger H. *How a Writer Works.* New York: Harper and Row, 1981.

Gibson, Walker. *Tough, Sweet, and Stuffy.* Bloomington, Indiana: Indiana University Press, 1966.

Graves, Donald H. *Balance the Basics: Let Them Write.* Ford Foundation Papers on Research About Learning, 1978.

Hirsch, Eric Donald. *The Philosophy of Composition.* Chicago: University of Chicago Press, 1978.

Judy, Stephen, and Susan Judy. *An Introduction to the Teaching of Writing.* New York: John Wiley, 1981.

Koch, Carol, and James M. Brazil. *Strategies for Teaching the Composition Process.* Urbana, Illinois: National Council of Teachers of English, 1978.

Moffett, James. *A Student-Centered Language Arts Program, K–13: A Handbook for Teachers.* Boston: Houghton Mifflin Co., 1968.

Moffett, James. *Teaching the Universe of Discourse.* Boston: Houghton Mifflin Co., 1968.

Odell, Lee. "The Process of Writing and the Process of Learning." *College Composition and Communication* 31 (February 1980): 42–50.

Paull, Michael. "Invention: Understanding and Relationship between Sensation, Perception and Concept Formation." *College Composition and Communication* 25 (May 1974): 205–209.

Perron, John D. "Thinking and Writing." *Language Arts* 54 (October 1977): 742–749.

*Pinar, William, Ed. *Curriculum Theorizing: The Reconceptualists.* Berkeley, California: McCutcheon Publishers, 1975.

*Postman, Neil. *Teaching as a Conserving Activity.* New York: Delacourte Press, 1979.

Rico, Gabriele Lusse, and Mary Frances Classett. *Balancing the Hemispheres: Brain Research and the Teaching of Writing.* Berkeley, California: Bay Area Writing Project No. 11, 1980.

Rohman, D. Gordon. "Pre-Writing: The Stage of Discovery in the Writing Process." *College Composition and Communication* 16 (May 1965): 106–112.

Rose, Mike. "Rigid Rules, Inflexible Plans, and the Stifling of Language: A Cognitivist Analysis of Writer's Block." *College Composition and Communication* 31 (December 1980): 389–400.

Throckmorton, Helen J. "Do Your Writing Assignments Work?—Checklist for a Good Writing Assignment." *English Journal* 69 (November 1980): 56–59.

Weaver, Constance. *Grammar for Teachers: Perspectives and Definitions.* Urbana, Illinois: National Council of Teachers of English, 1978.

THE BRITISH APPROACH

Adams, Parveen, Ed. *Language in Thinking.* 2nd ed. Hammondsworth, England: Penguin Books, 1973.

Applebee, Arthur H. "Writing Across the Curriculum: The London Projects." *English Journal* 66 (December 1977): 81–85.

Barnes, Douglas. *From Communication to Curriculum.* Montclair, New Jersey: Boynton/Cook Publishers, Inc., 1976.

Britton, James. *Writing to Learn, Learning to Write.* Urbana, Illinois: National Council of Teachers of English, 1972.

Britton, James, et al. *The Development of Writing Abilities, 11–18.* Urbana, Illinois: National Council of Teachers of English, 1975.

Bullock, Sir Alan, F.B.A., Chair, Committee of Inquiry Appointed for Education and Service. *A Language for Life* (called "The Bullock Report"). H.M.S.O., 1975.

Clay, Marie M. *What Did I Write?* London: Heinemann Educational Books, 1975.

Halliday, M.A.K. *Explorations in the Functions of Language.* New York: Elsevier Science Publishing Co., 1977.

Marland, Michael. *Language Across the Curriculum.* London: Heinemann, 1977.

Martin, Nancy. *Writing and Learning Across the Curriculum.* Montclair, New Jersey: Boynton/Cook Publishing, Inc., 1979.

Mollett, Margaret, and Pernard Newsome. *Talking, Writing and Learning.* Schools Council Report #59. London: Evans/Methuen Educational, 1977.

Nystrand, Martin, Ed. *Language as a Way of Knowing: A Book of Readings.* Ontario Institute for Studies in Education, 1977.

Parry, Christopher. *English Through Drama: A Way of Teaching.* Cambridge, England: University Press, 1972.

Rosen, Lois. "An Interview with James Britton, Tony Burgess, and Harold Rosen," *English Journal* 67 (November 1978): 5–58.

Taylor, John L., and Rex Walford. *Simulation in the Classroom.* Hammondsworth, England: Penguin Books, 1972.

THE CONNECTION BETWEEN WRITING AND LEARNING

*Anderson, Barry F. *Cognitive Psychology: The Study of Knowing, Learning, and Thinking.* New York: Academic Press, 1975.

*Bloom, Benjamin, Ed. *Taxonomy of Educational Objectives: The Classification of Educational Goals. Handbook I: The Cognitive Domain.* New York: David McKay, 1972.

*Bruner, Jerome. *Beyond the Information Given.* Berkeley, California: McCutcheon Publishing, 1973.

*Bruner, Jerome. *On Knowing: Essays for the Left Hand.* Cambridge: Harvard University Press, 1962.

Cherwitz, Richard. "Rhetoric as a Way of Knowing: An Attenuation of the Epistemological Claims of the 'New Rhetoric.'" *Southern Speech Communication Journal* 42 (Spring 1977): 207–219.

Collins, Terence, and Suzanne Hofer. "A Selected Annotated Bibliography of Articles on Interdepartmental Responsibility for the Teaching of Writing Skills." Report Prepared at the University of Minnesota, 1976.

Connelly, P.J., and D.C. Irving. "Composition and the Liberal Arts: A Shared Responsibility." *College English* 37 (March 1976): 668–670.

Donlan, Dan. "How to Involve Other Departments in Helping You Teach Writing." Paper presented at the National Convention of the National Council of Teachers of English, Chicago, November, 1976.

Donlan, Dan. "Teaching Writing in the Content Areas: Eleven Hypotheses from a Teacher Survey." *Research in the Teaching of English* 8 (Spring 1974): 250–262.

Draper, Virginia. *Formative Writing: Writing to Assist Learning in All Subject Areas.* Berkeley, California: Bay Area Writing Pamphlet No. 3, 1979.

Emig, Janet. "Writing as a Mode of Learning." *College Composition and Communication* 28 (May 1977): 122–128.

Flower, Linda. "Problem-Solving Strategies and the Writing Process." *College English* 39 (December 1977): 449–461.

Flower, Linda, and John R. Hayes. "The Cognition of Discovery: Defining a Rhetoric Problem." *College Composition and Communication* 31 (February 1980):21–32.

Freisinger, Randy. "Cross Disciplinary Writing Workshops: Theory and Practice." *College English* 42 (October 1980): 154–166.

Fulwiler, Toby. "Journal-Writing Across the Curriculum" in *Classroom Practices in Teaching English 1979–80: How to Handle the Paper Load.* Urbana, Illinois: National Council of Teachers of English, 1979.

Gere, Anne Ruggles. "Writing and Writing." *English Journal* 77 (November 1977): 60–64.

Gregg, L.W., and E.R. Stemberg, Eds. *Cognitive Processes in Writing.* Hillsdale, New Jersey: Erlbaum, 1980.

Hamilton, David. "Interdisciplinary Writing." *College English* 41 (March 1980): 780–796.

Herrington, Anne J. "Writing to Learn: Writing Across the Disciplines." *College English* 43 (April 1981): 379–387.

*Inhelder, Barbel, and Jean Piaget. *The Early Growth of Logic in the Child.* New York: W.W. Norton, 1969.

Irmscher, William F. "Writing as a Way of Learning and Developing." *College Composition and Communication* 30 (October 1979): 240–244.

Irmscher, William F. "The Teaching of Writing in Terms of Growth." *English Journal* 66 (December 1977): 33–36.

Jenkinson, Edward B., and Donald A. Seybold. *Writing as a Process of Discovery: Some Structured Theme Assignments.* Bloomington, Indiana: Indiana University Press, 1970.

Kroll, Barry M. "Developmental Perspectives and the Teaching of Composition." *College English* 41 (March 1980): 741–752.

Larson, Richard L. "English: An Enabling Discipline." *ADE Bulletin* 46 (September 1975): 3–7.

Maimon, Elaine, et al. *Writing in the Arts and Sciences.* New York: Winthrop, 1981.

*O'Neill, Hugh P., S.J. *Reasoning by Analogy.* Detroit: University of Detroit Press, 1967.

Pauk, Walter. *How to Study in College.* Boston: Houghton Mifflin Co., 1974.

Raimes, Ann. "Writing and Learning Across the Curriculum." *College English* 41 (March 1980): 797–801.

Rodgers, Paul C. "Breaching the Abstraction Barrier." *College Composition and Communication* 17 (February 1966): 24–28.

Scheffler, Judith A. "Composition with Content: An Interdisciplinary Approach." *College Composition and Communication* 31 (February 1980): 51–57.

Schorr, Ira. "Learning How to Learn: Conceptual Teaching in a Course called 'Utopia.'" *College English* 38 (March 1977): 64–74.

Smith, E. Brooks, Kenneth Goodman, and Robert Meredith. *Language and Thinking in the Elementary School.* New York: Holt, Rinehart and Winston, 1970.

Smith, Myrna J. "Bruner on Writing." *College Composition and Communication* 27 (May 1977): 129–133.

*Sperry, Len, Ed. *Learning Performance and Individual Differences.* Glenview, Illinois: Scott, Foresman and Co., 1972.

Vygotsky, Lev Semonovich. *Thought and Language.* Trans. Eugenia Hanfmann and Gertrude Vakar. Boston: MIT Press, 1975.

Wottring, Anne Miller. "Talking and Writing Across the Curriculum." Paper presented at the National Convention of the National Council of Teachers of English, Cincinnati, November, 1980.

CREATIVITY

*Adams, James L. *Conceptual Blockbusting.* San Francisco: W.H. Freeman, 1974.

Barrell, John. *Playgrounds of Our Minds.* New York: Teachers College Press, 1980.

Carlson, Ruth Kearney. *Writing Aids Through the Grades.* New York: Teachers College Press, 1970.

*Debono, Edward. *New Think.* New York: Basic Books, 1958.

Dehaven, Edna. "A Questioning Strategy Model for Creative Writing." *Elementary English* 50 (September 1973): 959–961, 987.

Ghiselin, Brewster. *The Creative Process: A Symposium.* New York: Mentor Books, 1952.

Koestler, Arthur. *The Act of Creation.* New York: Dell, 1967.

Koch, Kenneth. *Wishes, Lies, and Dreams.* New York: Chelsea House, 1970.

*Kuhn, Thomas. *The Structure of Scientific Revolutions.* Chicago: The University of Chicago Press, 1975.

Prince, George. *The Practice of Creativity.* New York: Harper and Row, 1970.

STUDENT INVOLVEMENT

Bergman, Floyd L. *The English Teacher's Activities Handbook: An Ideabook for Middle and Secondary Schools.* Boston: Allyn and Bacon, 1975.

Bruffee, Kenneth A. "Collaborative Learning: Some Practical Models." *College English* 34 (February 1973): 634–643.

Carlson, Ruth. *Writing Aids Through the Grades: One Hundred Eighty-Six Developmental Writing Activities.* New York: Teachers College Press, 1970.

Colburn, C. William. *Strategies for Educational Debate.* Boston: Holbrook Press, 1972.

Davis, Ken, and John Hollowell, Eds. *Inventing and Playing Games in the English Classroom.* Urbana, Illinois: National Council of Teachers of English, 1977.

Flavell, Jon H., et al. *The Development of Role-Taking and Communication Skills in Children.* New York: John Wiley, 1968.

Francoz, M.J. "The Logic of Questioning and Answering: Writing as Inquiry." *College English* 41 (November 1979): 336–339.

Friss, Dick. *Writing Class: Teacher and Students Writing Together.* Berkeley, California: Bay Area Writing Pamphlet No. 11, 1979.

Gillen, Caroline J. *Questioneze.* Columbus, Ohio: Merrill, 1972.

Goffe, Lewis C., and Nancy H. Deane. "Questioning Our Questions." *College Composition and Communication* 25 (October 1974): 284–291.

Graves, Richard L. *Rhetoric and Composition: A Sourcebook for Teachers.* Rochelle Park, New Jersey: Hayden, 1976.

Hawkins, Thom. *Group Inquiry Techniques for Teaching Writing.* Urbana, Illinois: National Council of Teachers of English, 1976.

Hoover, Kenneth. *The Professional Teacher's Handbook: A Guide for Improving Instruction in Today's Middle and Secondary Schools.* Boston: Allyn and Bacon, 1976.

Hunkins, Francis P. *Involving Students in Questioning.* Boston: Allyn and Bacon, 1976.

Judy, Stephen N. *Explorations in the Teaching of Secondary English: A Sourcebook for Experimental Teaching.* New York: Dodd, Mead and Co., 1975.

Kraus, W. Keith. *Murder, Mischief, and Mayhem: A Process for Creative Research Papers.* Urbana, Illinois: National Council of Teachers of English, 1978.

Raths, Louis, Herrill Harmin, and Sidney Simon. *Values and Teaching.* Columbus, Ohio: Charles E. Merrill, 1966.

*Read, Donald A., and Sidney B. Simon. *Humanistic Education Sourcebook.* New York: Prentice-Hall, 1975.

Sanders, Norris. *Classroom Questions: What Kinds?* New York: Harper and Row, 1966.

Spann, Sylvia, and Mary Beth Culp, Eds. *Thematic Units in Teaching English and the Humanities.* Urbana, Illinois: National Council of Teachers of English, 1975.

Stanford, Gene, Ed. *Classroom Practices in Teaching English, 1978–79: Activating the Passive Student.* Urbana, Illinois: National Council of Teachers of English, 1978.

Stanford, Gene, and Marie Smith. *A Guidebook for Teaching Composition.* Boston: Allyn and Bacon, 1978.

Styles, Ken, and Gray Cavanaugh. "Language Across the Curriculum: The Art of Questioning and Responding." *English Journal* 69 (February 1980): 24–27.

*Whitehead, Frank. *The Disappearing Dias.* London: Chatto and Windus, 1966.

REMEDIATION IN WRITING

Chaika, Elaine. "Who Can Be Taught?" *College English* 55 (February 1974): 575–583.

Fisher, Dexter, and Lois Larndin. "Libra: An Interdisciplinary Approach to Remediation." *ADE Bulletin* 41 (May 1979): 3–7.

Holbrook, David. *English for the Rejected.* Cambridge, England: Cambridge University Press, 1965.

Johnson, Sabina Thorne. "Remedial English: The Anglocentric Albatross." *College English* 33 (March 1972): 670–685.

Kroll, Barry M., and John C. Schafer. "Error Analysis and the Teaching of Composition." *College Composition and Communication* 29 (October 1978): 242–248.

Laurence, Patricia. "Error's Endless Train: Why Students Don't Perceive Errors." *Basic Writing* I (Spring 1975): 14–22.

*Lerner, Janet W. *Children with Learning Disabilities*. Boston: Houghton Mifflin Co., 1971.

Lloyd, Donald J. "Our National Mania for Correctness." *The American Scholar* 21 (Summer 1952): 283–289.

Lunsford, Andrea. "What We Know—and Don't Know—About Remedial Writing." *College Composition and Communication* 29 (February 1978): 47–52.

Lunsford, Andrea. "Cognitive Development and the Basic Writer." *College English* 41 (September 1979): 38–46.

Pinton, William H. "A Contemporary Dilemma: The Question of Standard English." *College Composition and Communication* 25 (October 1974): 247–251.

Shaughnessy, Mina P. "Diving In: An Introduction to Basic Writing." *College Composition and Communication* 27 (October 1976): 234–239.

Shaughnessy, Mina P. *Errors and Expectations*. New York: Oxford University Press, 1977.

Ylvisaker, Miriam. *An Experiment in Encouraging Fluency*. Berkeley, California: Bay Area Writing Project No. 8, 1979.

TESTING

*Buros, O.K. *The Seventh Annual Mental Measurement Yearbook*. Highland Park, New Jersey: The Gryphon Press, 1972.

Rudman, H.C. "Standardized Test Flap." *Phi Delta Kappan* 59 (March 1978): 470–471.

Taylor, W.S. "Cloze Procedures: A New Tool for Measuring Reading." *Journalism Quarterly* 30 (Fall 1953): 415–433.

Venable, T.C. "Declining SAT Scores: Some Unpopular Hypotheses." *Phi Delta Kappan* 62 (February 1981): 443–445.

GRADING

Cooper, Charles R., and Lee Odell. *Evaluating Writing: Describing, Measuring, Judging*. Urbana, Illinois: National Council of Teachers of English, 1978.

Corrington, David H., and Hugh F. Keedy. "A Technical Communication Course Using Peer Evaluation of Reports." *Engineering Education* 69 (February 1979): 417–419.

Diederich, Paul. *Measuring Growth in English*. Urbana, Illinois: National Council of Teachers of English, 1974.

Fassler, Barbara. "The Red Pen Revisited: Teaching Composition Through Student Conferences." *College English* 40 (October 1978): 186–190.

Ford, James E., and Gregory Larkin. "The Portfolio System: An End to Back-sliding Writing Standards." *College English* 39 (April 1978): 950–955.

Freedman, Sara. "Why Teachers Give the Grades They Do." *College Composition and Communication* 30 (May 1979): 161–164.

Healy, Mary K. *Using Student Writing Response Groups in the Classroom.* Berkeley, California: Bay Area Writing Pamphlet No. 12, 1980.

Holbrook, David. *Children's Writing: A Sampler for Student Teachers.* Cambridge, England: Cambridge University Press, 1967.

Judine, Sister M., IHM. *A Guide for Evaluating Student Compositions.* Urbana, Illinois: National Council of Teachers of English, 1965.

Lambers, Walter J. "Feedback on Writing: Much More Than Teacher Corrections." *Colorado Language Arts Society Journal* 12 (May 1977): 33–38.

Larson, Richard L. "The Whole Is More than the Sum of Its Parts: Notes on Responding to Students' Papers." *Arizona English Bulletin* 16 (1974): 175–181.

Odell, Lee. "Responding to Student Writing." *College Composition and Communication* 24 (December 1973): 393–400.

Palmer, Orville. "Seven Ways of Grading Dishonestly." *English Journal* 51 (October 1962): 464–469.

Searle, Dennis, and David Dillon. "Responding to Student Writing: What Is Said, or How It Is Said." *Language Arts* 57 (October 1980): 223–281.

Stanford, Gene. *Classroom Practices in Teaching English, 1979–80: How to Handle the Paper Load.* Urbana, Illinois: National Council of Teachers of English, 1979.

Stiff, Robert. "The Effect Upon Student Composition of Particular Correction Techniques." *Research in the Teaching of English* 1 (Spring 1967): 54–75.

Veit, Richard C. "De-Grading Composition: Do Papers Need Grades?" *College English* 41 (December 1979): 423–435.

WRITING AND READING

Ausubel, David P. "The Use of Advance Organizers in the Learning and Retention of Meaningful Verbal Material." *Journal of Educational Psychology* 51 (October 1960): 267–274.

Bechtel, Judith, and Bettie Franzblau. *Reading in the Science Classroom.* Washington, D.C.: National Education Association, 1980.

Bleich, David. *Readings and Feelings: An Introduction to Subjective Criticism.* Urbana, Illinois: National Council of Teachers of English, 1975.

Estes, Thomas H., and Joseph L. Vaughn. *Reading and Learning in the Content Classroom.* Boston: Allyn and Bacon, 1978.

Herber, Harold. *Teaching Reading in Content Areas.* Englewood Cliffs, New Jersey: Prentice-Hall, 1970.

Robinson, Francis P. *Effective Reading.* New York: Harper and Row, 1962.

Rosenblatt, Louise. *The Reader, the Text, the Poem.* Carbondale, Illinois: Southern Illinois University Press, 1978.

*Smith, Frank. *Psycholinguistics and Reading.* New York: Holt, Rinehart and Winston, 1973.

*Thomas, Ellen Lamar, and H. Alan Robinson. *Improving Reading in Every Class: A Sourcebook for Teachers,* 2nd ed. Boston: Allyn and Bacon, 1982.

Webb, Agnes J. "Transactions with Literary Texts: Conversations in Classrooms." *English Journal* 71 (March 1982): 56–60.

WRITING AND MATH

Kohl, Herbert R. *Math, Writing, and Games in the Open Classroom.* New York: Random House, 1974.

*Rising, Gerald R., and Richard A. Wiesen. *Mathematics in the Secondary School Classroom.* New York: Thomas Y. Crowell, 1972.

*Sawyer, W.W. *Mathematician's Delight.* Baltimore: Penguin Books, 1969.

WRITING, HISTORY, AND THE SOCIAL SCIENCES

*Berger, Peter. *Invitation to Sociology.* Garden City, New York: Anchor Books, 1963.

*Beyer, Barry. *Inquiry in the Social Studies Classroom: A Strategy for Teaching.* Columbus, Ohio: Charles E. Merrill, 1971.

Hoffman, Eleanor. "Writing for the Social Sciences." *College Composition and Communication* 28 (May 1977): 195–197.

*Kluckhohn, Clyde. *Mirror for Man.* New York: Whittlesey House, 1949.

Levy, Tedd, and Donna C. Krasnow. *Guidebook for Teaching U.S. History.* Boston: Allyn and Bacon, 1979.

*Long, Harold M., and Robert N. King. Improving the Teaching of World Affairs. Washington, D.C.: National Council for the Social Studies, 1964.

Newmann, Fred M., and Donald W. Oliver. "Case Approaches in Social Sciences." *Social Education* 31 (February 1967): 108–113.

Pigors, Paul, and Faith Pigors. *Case Method in Human Relations: The Incident Process.* New York: McGraw-Hill, 1961.

Weeks, Francis W. "How to Write Problems." *The ABCA Bulletin* 41 (June 1978): 20–22.

WRITING AND SCIENCE

Bowen, Mary Elizabeth, and Joseph A Mazzeo. *Writing About Science*. New York: Oxford University Press, 1979.

Burkett, David Warren. *Writing Science News for the Mass Media*. Houston: Gulf Publishing Co., 1965.

Carlisle, E. Fred. "Teaching Scientific Writing Humanistically: From Theory to Action." *English Journal* 67 (April 1978): 35–39.

Hamilton, David. "Writing Science." *College English* 40 (September 1978): 32–40.

*Hurd, Paul de Hart. *New Directions in Teaching Secondary School Science*. Chicago: Rand McNally, 1971.

Maxwell, Rhoda, and Stephen Judy. "Science Writing in an English Classroom." *English Journal* 67 (April 1978): 78–81.

McKinnon, Joe W. "Encouraging Logical Thinking in Selected Pre-Engineering Students." *Engineering Education* 66 (April 1976): 74–84.

*Morholt, Evelyn, Paul F. Brandwein, and Joseph Alexander. *A Sourcebook for the Biological Sciences*. 2nd ed. New York: Harcourt, Brace and World, Inc., 1966.

Pella, Milton O. "Concept Learning in Science." *The Science Teacher* 33 (December 1966): 31–34.

Index

the focus of objective tests, 181; mentioned, 5, 6, 38, 153. *See also* Accuracy; Errors in writing; Process in writing; Proofreading symbols

Egocentrism: discussion of, 8, 41, 146, 147, 157; in poetic writing, 149. *See also* Idiosyncracies

Emotion: as a factor in writing, 4, 5, 14, 134, 135, 141, 144

Encyclopedias: why not to use, 82–83

English class: assignments, 124, 133, 139–140, 158–159, 181, 183; mentioned, 11, 94. *See also* Literature class

Errors in writing: described, 6, 30–58 *passim*; alternatives to marking, 157–164; as a sign of growth, 79–80, 133, 161; how much to count in grading, 91, 106, 113–114, 125–128, 152–155, 156, 160–161, 167–169, 171–172; as a block to discussion, 182. *See also* Grading

Essay tests, 113–129, 164, 169. *See also* Creativity; Grading; Topics

Essays, 16, 19

Evaluation. *See* Grading

Expository writing. *See* Transactional writing

Expressive writing: defined, 12, 16, 20; its place in all coursework, 13–15, 17, 18, 20–28, 58–59, 72–73; sample of, 74; in case studies, 99; in debates, 100–101, 104; on essay tests, 121; as precursor of poetic writing, 133, 138; appropriate response to, 12, 156, 157, 164

Fantasy, 133

Fear of writing. *See* Anxiety about writing

Fiction. *See* Poetic writing

Figurative language. *See* Metaphor

Films, 112, 144, 146

Fluency, 12, 17

Formality. *See* Tone

Free writings, defined, 17. *See also* Expressive writing

Generalizations. *See* Abstract thinking

Geography class, 72, 97, 139–140. *See also* History class; Science class; Social studies class

Goals in writing, 7, 28, 180

Government class, 11, 37–38, 81, 87, 99. *See also* Social studies class

Grading: what to look for, 2, 25, 106–111, 147, 148, 152–180; effect on morale, 113, 114, 120, 124–129, 134; subjectivity in, 128–129; of journals, 73; of debates, 103; of research papers, 87, 92, 106, 107–110, 164–167, 169; of essay tests, 124–129; of poetic writing, 147–149; effect on morale, 128–129, 155, 171, 179, 180. *See also* Checklists; Comments on student writing; Responses to writing

Grammar, 4, 19, 32, 41, 88, 92, 142, 159–161

Graphs, 41–43, 138–140

Group work: discussions, 26–28, 49, 51, 59, 75–76; with case studies, 99; with debates, 100–105; with essay test-taking, 119–121; in preparing poetic writing, 138, 144; in responding to writing, 76, 87–89, 90–91, 148, 157, 162–165; use of checklists with, 164–167; mentioned, 34, 37, 85, 117, 177

Haiku, 141–143

Handwriting, 125, 175

Hemispheres of the brain, 134–135, 150

History class: writing, 53–55, 64, 66–67, 72, 94, 97, 99, 121, 122–123, 136, 139–140, 142, 145, 146–147; mentioned, 13, 159, 181

Holistic evaluation, 125–126, 169

Hypercorrection, 126, 159, 160–161